BILINGUAL
VISUAL
DICTIONARY

BILINGUAL VISUAL DICTIONARY

FIRST EDITION
Senior Editors Angeles Gavira, Angela Wilkes
Senior Art Editor Ina Stradins
Designed for DK by WaltonCreative.com
Language content for DK by g-and-w publishing

REVISED EDITION

DK LONDON
Senior Editor Christine Stroyan
Project Editor Sophie Adam
Designer Thomas Keenes
Managing Editor Carine Tracanelli
Managing Art Editor Anna Hall
Senior Production Controllers Poppy David, Meskerem Berhane
Senior Jacket Designer Surabhi Wadhwa Gandhi
Jacket Design Development Manager Sophia MTT
Translations by Andiamo! Language Services Ltd
Art Editor Karen Self
Associate Publishing Director Liz Wheeler
Publishing Director Jonathan Metcalf

DK INDIA
Editor Alka Thakur-Hazarika
Desk Editors Pankhoori Sinha, Joicy John
DTP Designers Anurag Trivedi, Rakesh Sharma
Assistant Picture Researchers Geetam Biswas, Shubhdeep Kaur
Senior Art Editor Vikas Chauhan
Managing Editor Saloni Singh
Managing Art Editor Govind Mittal
DTP Coordinator Tarun Sharma
Preproduction Manager Balwant Singh
Senior Jacket Coordinator Priyanka Sharma Saddi

DK US
US Proofreader Chuck Hutchinson
US Executive Editor Lori Cates Hand

This American Edition, 2024
First American Edition, 2005
Published in the United States by DK Publishing,
a division of Penguin Random House LLC
1745 Broadway, 20th Floor, New York, NY 10019

**The corresponding free audio is available for a period of at least
5 years from publication of this edition.**

Printed and bound in China

www.dk.com

MIX
Paper | Supporting
responsible forestry
FSC™ C018179

This book was made with Forest
Stewardship Council™ certified
paper — one small step in DK's
commitment to a sustainable future.
Learn more at
www.dk.com/uk/information/sustainability

table des matières
contents

à propos du dictionnaire
about the dictionary

comment utiliser ce livre
how to use this book

les gens
people

l'apparence
appearance

la maison
home

les services
services

les courses
shopping

la nourriture
food

l'éducation
study

le travail
work

le transport
transportation

les sports
sports

l'environnement
environment

l'information
reference

index
indexes

remerciements
acknowledgments

à propos du dictionnaire

Il est bien connu que les illustrations nous aident à comprendre et retenir l'information. Fondé sur ce principe, ce dictionnaire bilingue richement illustré présente un large éventail de vocabulaire courant et utile dans deux langues européennes.

Le dictionnaire est divisé de façon thématique et couvre en détail la plupart des aspects du monde quotidien.

Il s'agit d'un outil de référence essentiel pour tous ceux qui s'intéressent aux langues—pratique, stimulant et d'emploi facile.

Quelques points à noter

Les deux langues sont toujours présentées dans le même ordre—français et anglais.

En français, les noms sont donnés avec leurs articles définis qui indiquent leur genre (masculin ou féminin) et leur nombre (singulier ou pluriel). L'article défini est "le" pour les noms masculins, "la" pour les noms féminins et "les" pour les noms pluriels. Exemples :

le frère
brother

la graine   **les amandes**
seed   almonds

Le genre des adjectifs, personnes et métiers est indiqué par lettre *m* (masculin) ou *f* (féminin).

frais *m*   **l'avocat** *m*
fraîche *f*   **l'avocate** *f*
fresh   lawyer

Les verbes sont indiqués par un (v), par exemple:

récolter | harvest (v)

Chaque langue a également son propre index à la fin du livre. Vous pourrez y vérifier un mot dans n'importe laquelle des deux langues et vous serez renvoyé au(x) numéro(s) de(s) page(s) où il figure. Le genre des mots est signalé à l'aide de la lettre *m* ou *f*.

comment utiliser ce livre

Que vous appreniez une nouvelle langue pour les affaires, le plaisir ou pour préparer vos vacances, ou encore si vous espérez élargir votre vocabulaire dans une langue qui vous est déjà familière, ce dictionnaire sera pour vous un outil d'apprentissage précieux que vous pourrez utiliser de plusieurs manières.

Lorsque vous apprenez une nouvelle langue, recherchez les mots apparentés (mots qui se ressemblent dans différentes langues) et les faux amis (mots qui se ressemblent mais ont des significations nettement différentes). Par exemple, l'anglais a importé des autres langues européennes de nombreux termes désignant la nourriture mais, en retour, exporté des termes employés dans le domaine de la technologie et de la culture populaire.

Activités pratiques d'apprentissage

• Lorsque vous vous déplacez dans votre maison, au travail ou à l'université, essayez de regarder les pages qui correspondent à ce contexte. Vous pouvez ensuite fermer le livre, regarder autour de vous et voir combien d'objets vous pouvez nommer.

• Forcez-vous à écrire une histoire, une lettre ou un dialogue en employant le plus de termes possibles choisis dans une page. Ceci vous aidera à retenir le vocabulaire et son orthographe. Si vous souhaitez pouvoir écrire un texte plus long, commencez par des phrases qui incorporent 2 à 3 mots.

• Si vous avez une mémoire très visuelle, essayez de dessiner ou de décalquer des objets du livre sur une feuille de papier, puis fermez le livre et inscrivez les mots sous l'image.

• Une fois que vous serez plus sûr de vous, choisissez des mots dans l'index de la langue étrangère et essayez de voir ce que vous en connaissez le sens avant de vous reporter à la page correspondante pour vérifier.

application audio gratuite

L'application audio contient tous les mots et les phrases du livre, prononcés en anglais et en français par des natifs des deux langues, afin de faciliter la maîtrise d'un vocabulaire essentiel, et aider à améliorer la prononciation. Le contenu audio est également proposé pour tous les autres livres de la série.

comment utiliser l'application audio?

• Recherchez "DK Visual Dictionary" dans l'app store de votre choix et téléchargez gratuitement l'application sur votre smartphone ou tablette.
• Ouvrez l'application et sélectionnez la version de votre livre.
• Trouvez votre livre dans le menu "Choose your book" (Choisissez votre livre).
• Sélectionnez un chapitre dans la table des matières ou saisissez un numéro de page dans la barre de recherche.
• Triez les mots par ordre alphabétique en français ou en anglais.
• Explorez la liste pour trouver un mot ou une expression.
• Appuyez sur un mot pour écouter sa prononciation.

about the dictionary

The use of pictures is proven to aid understanding and the retention of information. Working on this principle, this highly illustrated bilingual dictionary presents a large range of useful current vocabulary in two European languages.

The dictionary is divided thematically and covers most aspects of the everyday world in detail.

This is an essential reference tool for anyone interested in languages—practical, stimulating, and easy-to-use.

A few things to note

The two languages are always presented in the same order—French and English.

In French, nouns are given with their definite articles reflecting the gender (masculine or feminine) and number (singular or plural). The definite article is "le" for a masculine noun, "la" for a feminine noun, and "les" for a plural noun; for example:

le frère
brother

la graine   **les amandes**
seed   almonds

Adjectives and words for people and professions are indicated with *m* for masculine and *f* for feminine.

frais *m*   **l'avocat** *m*
fraîche *f*   **l'avocate** *f*
fresh   lawyer

Verbs are indicated by a (v), for example:

récolter | harvest (v)

Each language also has its own index at the back of the book. Here you can look up a word in either of the two languages and be referred to the page number(s) where it appears. The gender is indicated with *m* or *f*.

how to use this book

Whether you are learning a new language for business, pleasure, or in preparation for a holiday abroad, or are hoping to extend your vocabulary in an already familiar language, this dictionary is a valuable learning tool which you can use in a number of different ways.

When learning a new language, look out for cognates (words that are alike in different languages) and false friends (words that look alike but carry significantly different meanings). You can also see where the languages have influenced each other. For example, English has imported many terms for food from other European languages but, in turn, exported terms used in technology and popular culture.

Practical learning activities

• As you move about your home, workplace, or college, try looking at the pages which cover that setting. You could then close the book, look around you and see how many of the objects and features you can name.

• Challenge yourself to write a story, letter, or dialogue using as many of the terms on a particular page as possible. This will help you retain the vocabulary and remember the spelling. If you want to build up to writing a longer text, start with sentences incorporating 2–3 words.

• If you have a very visual memory, try drawing or tracing items from the book onto a piece of paper, then close the book and fill in the words below the picture.

• Once you are more confident, pick out words in a foreign-language index and see if you know what they mean before turning to the relevant page to check if you were right.

free audio app

The DK Visual Dictionary app contains all the words and phrases in the book, spoken by native speakers in both French and English, making it easier to learn important vocabulary and improve your pronunciation. Audio is also available for all the other books in the series.

how to use the audio app

• Search for "DK Visual Dictionary" in you chosen app store and download the free app on your smartphone or table.

• Open the app and select your edition of the book.

• Select your book from the "Choose your book" menu.

• Select a chapter from the contents list or enter a page number in the search bar.

• Sort the words A–Z in French or English.

• Scroll up or down through the list to find a word or phrase.

• Tap a word to hear it.

les gens
people

le corps • body

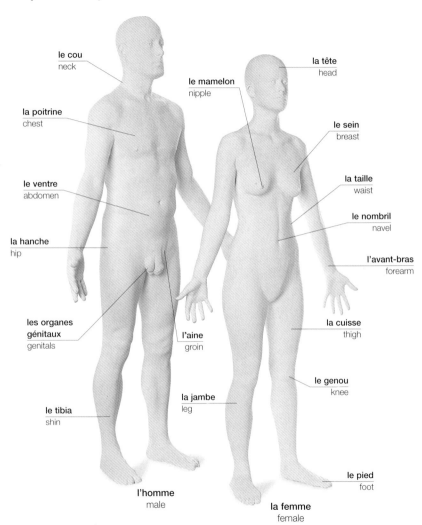

le cou
neck

le mamelon
nipple

la tête
head

la poitrine
chest

le sein
breast

la taille
waist

le ventre
abdomen

le nombril
navel

la hanche
hip

l'avant-bras
forearm

les organes
génitaux
genitals

l'aine
groin

la cuisse
thigh

le genou
knee

le tibia
shin

la jambe
leg

le pied
foot

l'homme
male

la femme
female

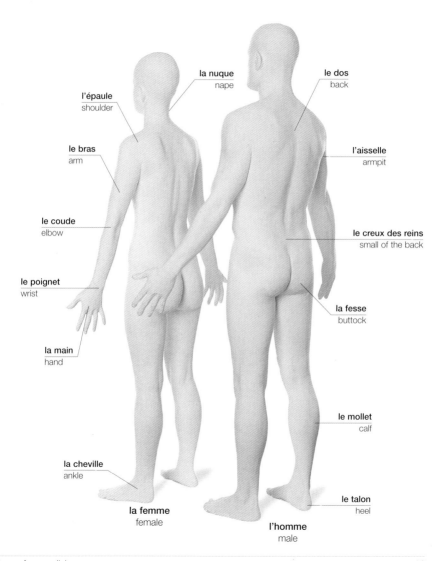

la nuque
nape

le dos
back

l'épaule
shoulder

le bras
arm

l'aisselle
armpit

le coude
elbow

le creux des reins
small of the back

le poignet
wrist

la fesse
buttock

la main
hand

le mollet
calf

la cheville
ankle

le talon
heel

la femme
female

l'homme
male

le visage • face

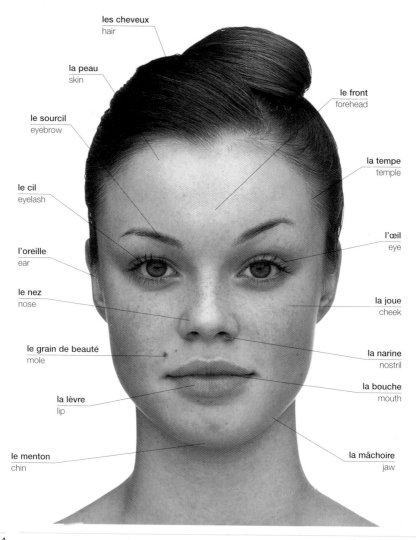

les cheveux
hair

la peau
skin

le sourcil
eyebrow

le cil
eyelash

l'oreille
ear

le nez
nose

le grain de beauté
mole

la lèvre
lip

le menton
chin

le front
forehead

la tempe
temple

l'œil
eye

la joue
cheek

la narine
nostril

la bouche
mouth

la mâchoire
jaw

la ride
wrinkle

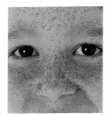
la tache de rousseur
freckle

le pore
pore

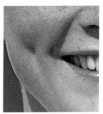
la fossette
dimple

la main • hand

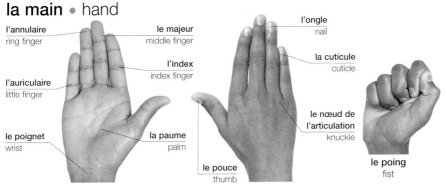

l'annulaire
ring finger

le majeur
middle finger

l'index
index finger

l'auriculaire
little finger

le poignet
wrist

la paume
palm

l'ongle
nail

la cuticule
cuticle

le nœud de l'articulation
knuckle

le pouce
thumb

le poing
fist

le pied • foot

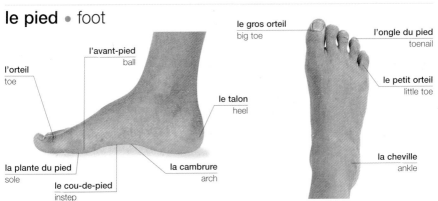

l'avant-pied
ball

l'orteil
toe

le talon
heel

la plante du pied
sole

le cou-de-pied
instep

la cambrure
arch

le gros orteil
big toe

l'ongle du pied
toenail

le petit orteil
little toe

la cheville
ankle

les muscles • muscles

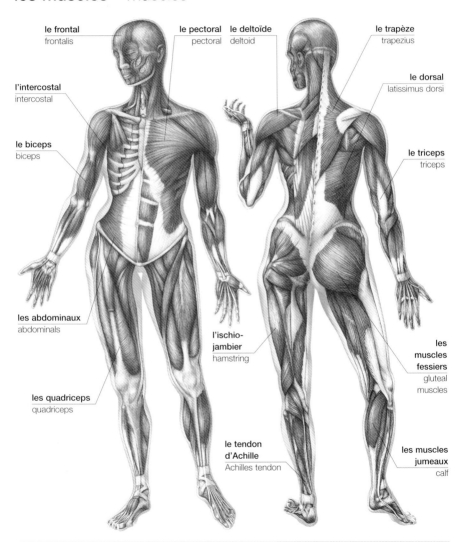

le frontal
frontalis

le pectoral
pectoral

le deltoïde
deltoid

le trapèze
trapezius

l'intercostal
intercostal

le dorsal
latissimus dorsi

le biceps
biceps

le triceps
triceps

les abdominaux
abdominals

l'ischio-
jambier
hamstring

les
muscles
fessiers
gluteal
muscles

les quadriceps
quadriceps

le tendon
d'Achille
Achilles tendon

les muscles
jumeaux
calf

le squelette • skeleton

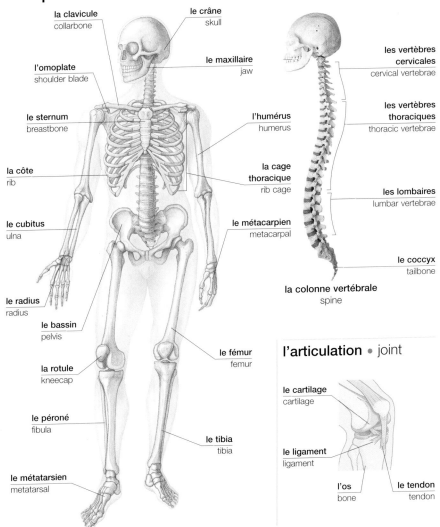

la clavicule
collarbone

le crâne
skull

l'omoplate
shoulder blade

le maxillaire
jaw

le sternum
breastbone

l'humérus
humerus

la côte
rib

la cage
thoracique
rib cage

le cubitus
ulna

le métacarpien
metacarpal

le radius
radius

le bassin
pelvis

la rotule
kneecap

le fémur
femur

le péroné
fibula

le tibia
tibia

le métatarsien
metatarsal

les vertèbres
cervicales
cervical vertebrae

les vertèbres
thoraciques
thoracic vertebrae

les lombaires
lumbar vertebrae

le coccyx
tailbone

la colonne vertébrale
spine

l'articulation • joint

le cartilage
cartilage

le ligament
ligament

l'os
bone

le tendon
tendon

les organes internes • internal organs

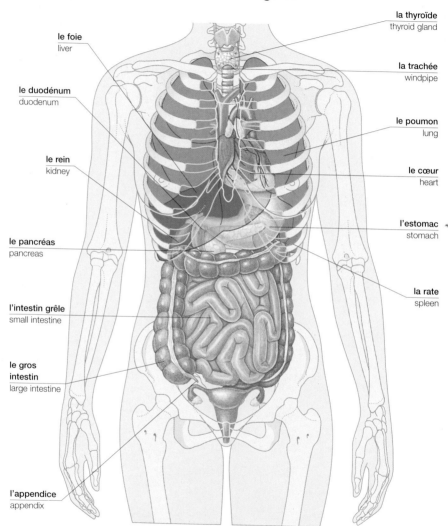

le foie
liver

le duodénum
duodenum

le rein
kidney

le pancréas
pancreas

l'intestin grêle
small intestine

**le gros
intestin**
large intestine

l'appendice
appendix

la thyroïde
thyroid gland

la trachée
windpipe

le poumon
lung

le cœur
heart

l'estomac
stomach

la rate
spleen

la tête • head

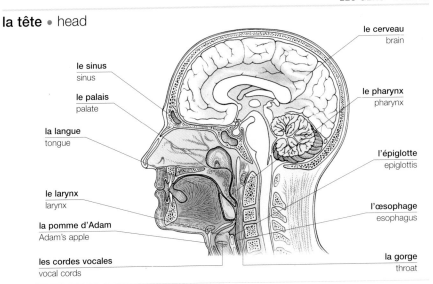

le cerveau
brain

le sinus
sinus

le palais
palate

la langue
tongue

le pharynx
pharynx

le larynx
larynx

l'épiglotte
epiglottis

la pomme d'Adam
Adam's apple

l'œsophage
esophagus

les cordes vocales
vocal cords

la gorge
throat

les systèmes du corps • body systems

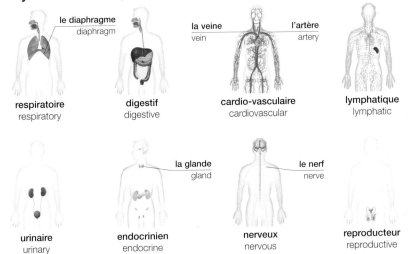

le diaphragme
diaphragm

la veine
vein

l'artère
artery

respiratoire
respiratory

digestif
digestive

cardio-vasculaire
cardiovascular

lymphatique
lymphatic

la glande
gland

le nerf
nerve

urinaire
urinary

endocrinien
endocrine

nerveux
nervous

reproducteur
reproductive

français • english

les organes de reproduction • reproductive organs

la trompe de Fallope
fallopian tube

le follicule
follicle

l'ovaire
ovary

la vessie
bladder

l'utérus
uterus

le clitoris
clitoris

le col de l'utérus
cervix

l'urètre
urethra

le vagin
vagina

les lèvres
labia

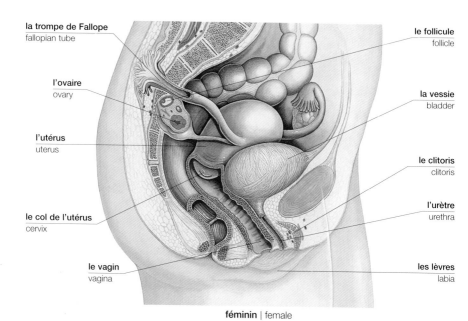

féminin | female

la reproduction
reproduction

le spermatozoïde
sperm

l'ovule
egg

la fertilisation | fertilization

vocabulaire • vocabulary

l'hormone hormone	**impuissant** impotent	**les règles** menstruation
l'ovulation ovulation	**fécond** fertile	**les rapports sexuels** intercourse
stérile infertile	**concevoir** conceive	**l'infection sexuellement transmissible** sexually transmitted infection

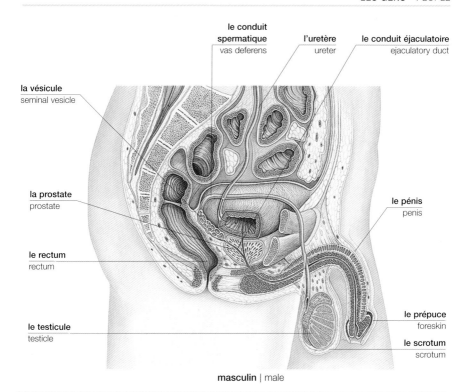

le conduit spermatique
vas deferens

l'uretère
ureter

le conduit éjaculatoire
ejaculatory duct

la vésicule
seminal vesicle

la prostate
prostate

le pénis
penis

le rectum
rectum

le testicule
testicle

le prépuce
foreskin

le scrotum
scrotum

masculin | male

la contraception • contraception

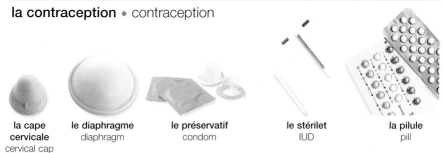

la cape cervicale
cervical cap

le diaphragme
diaphragm

le préservatif
condom

le stérilet
IUD

la pilule
pill

la famille • family

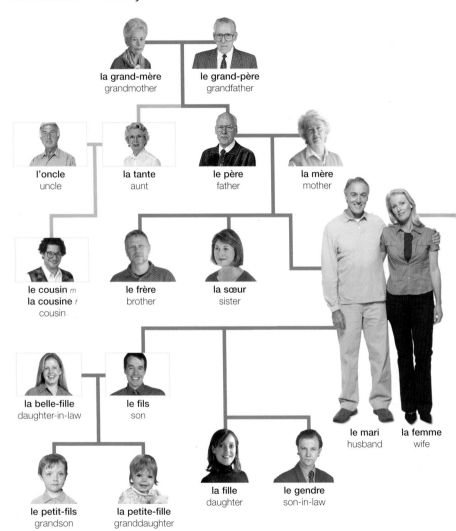

la grand-mère
grandmother

le grand-père
grandfather

l'oncle
uncle

la tante
aunt

le père
father

la mère
mother

le cousin *m*
la cousine *f*
cousin

le frère
brother

la sœur
sister

la belle-fille
daughter-in-law

le fils
son

le mari
husband

la femme
wife

le petit-fils
grandson

la petite-fille
granddaughter

la fille
daughter

le gendre
son-in-law

vocabulaire • vocabulary

les membres de la famille relatives	**les parents** parents	**les petits-enfants** grandchildren	**la belle-mère** stepmother	**le beau-fils** stepson	**la génération** generation
les grands-parents grandparents	**les enfants** children	**le beau-père** stepfather	**la belle-fille** stepdaughter	**le partenaire** m **la partenaire** f partner	**les jumeaux** m **les jumelles** f twins

la belle-mère
mother-in-law

le beau-père
father-in-law

le beau-frère
brother-in-law

la belle-sœur
sister-in-law

la nièce
niece

le neveu
nephew

les titres • titles

Madame
Mrs. / Ms.

Monsieur
Mr.

Mademoiselle
Miss

les stades • stages

le bébé m/f
baby

l'enfant m/f
child

le garçon
boy

la fille
girl

l'adolescent m
l'adolescente f
teenager

l'adulte m/f
adult

l'homme
man

la femme
woman

les relations • relationships

le responsable *m*	l'assistant *m*	l'associé *m*		l'employé *m*	le collègue *m*
la responsable *f*	l'assistante *f*	l'associée *f*	l'employeur *m/f*	l'employée *f*	la collègue *f*
manager	assistant	business partner	employer	employee	colleague

le bureau | office

le voisin *m*	l'ami *m*	la connaissance *m/f*	le correspondant *m*
la voisine *f*	l'amie *f*	acquaintance	la correspondante *f*
neighbor	friend		penpal

| le petit ami | la petite amie | le fiancé | la fiancée |
| boyfriend | girlfriend | fiancé | fiancée |

le couple | couple   les fiancés | engaged couple

les émotions • emotions

le sourire
smile

heureux *m*
heureuse *f*
happy

triste *m/f*
sad

excité *m*
excitée *f*
excited

ennuyé *m*
ennuyée *f*
bored

surpris *m*
surprise *f*
surprised

effrayé *m*
effrayée *f*
scared

**le froncement
de sourcils**
frown

fâché *m*
fâchée *f*
angry

perplexe *m/f*
confused

inquiet *m*
inquiète *f*
worried

nerveux *m*
nerveuse *f*
nervous

fier *m*
fière *f*
proud

confiant *m*
confiante *f*
confident

gêné *m*
gênée *f*
embarrassed

timide *m/f*
shy

vocabulaire • vocabulary

contrarié *m* / **contrariée** *f*
upset

choqué *m* / **choquée** *f*
shocked

rire laugh (v)

pleurer cry (v)

soupirer sigh (v)

s'évanouir faint (v)

crier shout (v)

bâiller yawn (v)

les événements de la vie • life events

naître
be born (v)

commencer à l'école
start school (v)

se faire des amis
make friends (v)

obtenir son diplôme
graduate (v)

trouver un emploi
get a job (v)

tomber amoureux *m*
tomber amoureuse *f*
fall in love (v)

se marier
get married (v)

avoir un bébé
have a baby (v)

le mariage | wedding

le divorce
divorce

l'enterrement
funeral

vocabulaire • vocabulary

le baptême christening	**mourir** die (v)
la bar-mitsvah bar mitzvah	**faire son testament** make a will (v)
l'anniversaire de mariage anniversary	**l'acte de naissance** birth certificate
émigrer emigrate (v)	**le repas de noces** wedding reception
prendre sa retraite retire (v)	**le voyage de noces** honeymoon

les fêtes • celebrations

la fête
birthday party

la carte
card

le cadeau
present

l'anniversaire
birthday

Noël
Christmas

les fêtes
festivals

Pessah
Passover

le Nouvel An
New Year

le carnaval
carnival

le défilé
procession

l'Aïd
Eid

le ruban
ribbon

la fête de Thanksgiving
Thanksgiving

Pâques
Easter

Halloween
Halloween

Diwali
Diwali

l'apparence
appearance

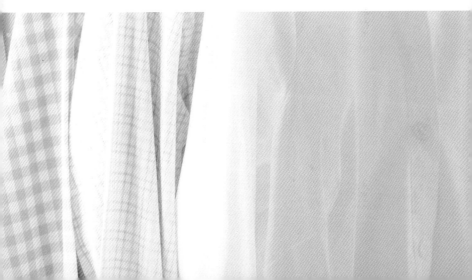

les vêtements d'enfants • children's clothing

le bébé *m/f* • baby

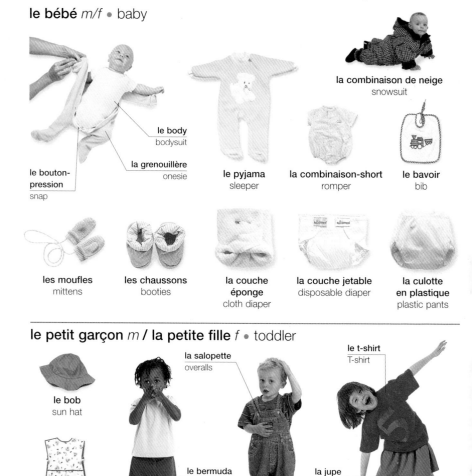

la combinaison de neige
snowsuit

le body
bodysuit

la grenouillère
onesie

le bouton-pression
snap

le pyjama
sleeper

la combinaison-short
romper

le bavoir
bib

les moufles
mittens

les chaussons
booties

la couche éponge
cloth diaper

la couche jetable
disposable diaper

la culotte en plastique
plastic pants

le petit garçon *m* / la petite fille *f* • toddler

la salopette
overalls

le t-shirt
T-shirt

le bob
sun hat

le tablier
apron

le bermuda
shorts

la jupe
skirt

l'enfant *m/f* • child

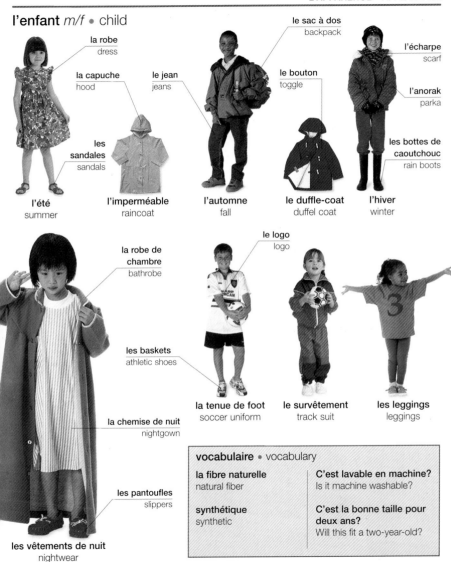

la robe
dress

la capuche
hood

le jean
jeans

les sandales
sandals

l'été
summer

l'imperméable
raincoat

le sac à dos
backpack

le bouton
toggle

l'automne
fall

le duffle-coat
duffel coat

l'écharpe
scarf

l'anorak
parka

les bottes de caoutchouc
rain boots

l'hiver
winter

la robe de chambre
bathrobe

les baskets
athletic shoes

la chemise de nuit
nightgown

les pantoufles
slippers

les vêtements de nuit
nightwear

le logo
logo

la tenue de foot
soccer uniform

le survêtement
track suit

les leggings
leggings

vocabulaire • vocabulary

la fibre naturelle natural fiber	**C'est lavable en machine?** Is it machine washable?
synthétique synthetic	**C'est la bonne taille pour deux ans?** Will this fit a two-year-old?

les vêtements • clothes (1)

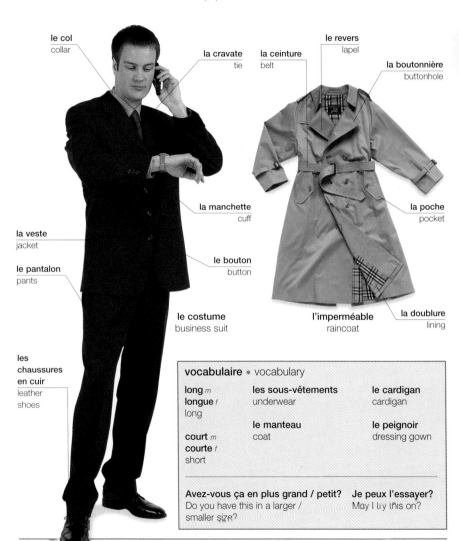

le col
collar

la cravate
tie

la ceinture
belt

le revers
lapel

la boutonnière
buttonhole

la manchette
cuff

la veste
jacket

le pantalon
pants

le bouton
button

la poche
pocket

les chaussures en cuir
leather shoes

le costume
business suit

l'imperméable
raincoat

la doublure
lining

vocabulaire • vocabulary

long *m* **longue** *f* long	**les sous-vêtements** underwear	**le cardigan** cardigan
court *m* **courte** *f* short	**le manteau** coat	**le peignoir** dressing gown

Avez-vous ça en plus grand / petit?
Do you have this in a larger / smaller size?

Je peux l'essayer?
May I try this on?

le blazer
blazer

la veste de sport
sport coat

le gilet
vest

l'encolure en V
V-neck

le col rond
crew neck

le t-shirt
T-shirt

l'anorak
parka

le sweat-shirt
sweatshirt

la chemise
shirt

le jean
jeans

le pullover
sweater

le pyjama
pajamas

le tricot de corps
undershirt

les vêtements décontractés
casual wear

le short
shorts

le slip
briefs

le caleçon
boxer shorts

les chaussettes
socks

les vêtements • clothes (2)

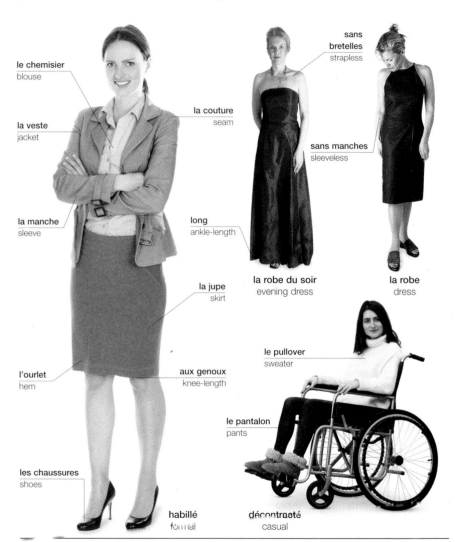

le chemisier
blouse

la couture
seam

la veste
jacket

sans bretelles
strapless

sans manches
sleeveless

la manche
sleeve

long
ankle-length

la robe du soir
evening dress

la robe
dress

la jupe
skirt

le pullover
sweater

aux genoux
knee-length

l'ourlet
hem

le pantalon
pants

les chaussures
shoes

habillé
formal

décontracté
casual

la lingerie • lingerie

le peignoir
robe

le fond de robe
slip

la bretelle
strap

la camisole
camisole

les porte-
jarretelles
garter straps

la guêpière
bustier

le bas
stocking

le collant
panty hose

le soutien-gorge
bra

le slip
panties

la chemise de nuit
nightgown

le mariage • wedding

le bouquet
bouquet

la robe de mariée
wedding dress

---

vocabulaire • vocabulary

le corset corset	**ajusté** tailored
la jarretière garter	**la ceinture** waistband
l'épaulette shoulder pad	**dos-nu** halter neck
le soutien-gorge de sport sports bra	**la dentelle** lace
à armature underwire	**le voile** veil

---

les accessoires • accessories

la casquette
cap

le chapeau
hat

le foulard
scarf

la boucle
buckle

la ceinture
belt

le manche
handle

la pointe
tip

le mouchoir
handkerchief

le nœud papillon
bow tie

l'épingle de cravate
tiepin

les gants
gloves

le parapluie
umbrella

les bijoux • jewelry

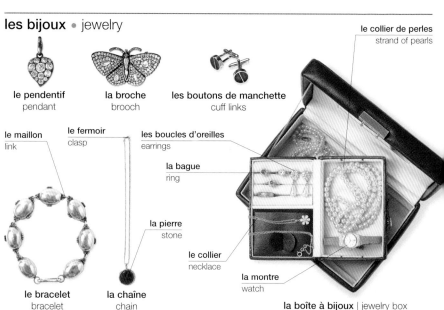

le pendentif
pendant

la broche
brooch

les boutons de manchette
cuff links

le collier de perles
strand of pearls

le maillon
link

le fermoir
clasp

les boucles d'oreilles
earrings

la bague
ring

la pierre
stone

le collier
necklace

la montre
watch

le bracelet
bracelet

la chaîne
chain

la boîte à bijoux | jewelry box

les sacs • bags

le fermoir
clasp

la bretelle
shoulder strap

les anses
handles

le portefeuille
wallet

le porte-monnaie
change purse

le sac à bandoulière
shoulder bag

le fourre-tout
duffel bag

la serviette
briefcase

le sac à main
handbag

le sac à dos
backpack

les chaussures • shoes

le lacet
lace

la languette
tongue

l'œillet
eyelet

la semelle
sole

la chaussure lacée
lace-up

le talon
heel

la botte
boot

la chaussure de marche
hiking boot

la basket
sneaker

la tong
flip-flop

la chaussure de cuir
dress shoe

la chaussure à talon haut
high-heeled shoe

la chaussure compensée
wedge

la sandale
sandal

le mocassin
slip-on

la ballerine
flat

les cheveux • hair

le peigne
comb

peigner
comb (v)

la brosse
brush

brosser | brush (v)

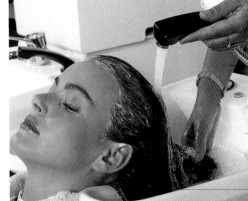

le coiffeur *m*
la coiffeuse *f*
hairdresser

le lavabo
sink

le client *m*
la cliente *f*
client

laver | wash (v)

le peignoir
robe

rincer
rinse (v)

couper
cut (v)

sécher
blow-dry (v)

faire une mise en plis
set (v)

les accessoires • accessories

le
sèche-
cheveux
blow-dryer

le shampoing
shampoo

l'après-shampoing
conditioner

le gel
gel

la laque
hairspray

le fer à friser
curling iron

les ciseaux
scissors

le serre-tête
headband

le fer à lisser
hair straightener

l'épingle à cheveux
bobby pins

les coiffures • styles

la queue de cheval
ponytail

la natte
braid

le chignon banane
French twist

le chignon
bun

les couettes
pigtails

le carré
bob

la coupe courte
short haircut

frisé
curly

la permanente
perm

raide
straight

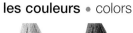
les racines
roots

les mèches
highlights

chauve
bald

la perruque
wig

---

vocabulaire • vocabulary

rafraîchir trim (v)	**sec** dry
lisser straighten (v)	**gras** greasy
les fourches split ends	**normal** normal
le coiffeur barber	**le cuir chevelu** scalp
les pellicules dandruff	**la barbe** beard
l'élastique pour cheveux hair tie	**la moustache** mustache

les couleurs • colors

blond *m* / **blonde** *f*
blond / blonde

châtain
brunette

auburn
auburn

roux
red

noir
black

gris
gray

blanc
white

teint
dyed

---

la beauté • beauty

la teinture de cheveux
hair dye

le fard à
paupières
eye shadow

le mascara
mascara

l'eye-liner
eyeliner

le fard à joues
blush

le fond de teint
foundation

le rouge à lèvres
lipstick

le maquillage • makeup

le crayon à sourcils
eyebrow pencil

la brosse à sourcils
eyebrow brush

la pince à épiler
tweezers

le brillant à lèvres
lip gloss

le pinceau à lèvres
lip brush

le crayon à lèvres
lip liner

le pinceau
brush

le correcteur
concealer

le miroir
mirror

la poudre
face powder

la houppette
powder puff

le poudrier | compact

les soins esthétiques
beauty treatments

le masque
face mask

l'épilation au fil
threading

le soin du visage
facial

exfolier
exfoliate (v)

l'épilation
wax

la pédicure
pedicure

les accessoires de toilette
toiletries

le démaquillant
cleanser

le tonique
toner

la crème
hydratante
moisturizer

l'autobronzant
self-tanning lotion

le parfum
perfume

l'eau de toilette
eau de toilette

la manucure • manicure

le dissolvant
nail polish remover

la lime à ongles
nail file

le vernis à ongles
nail polish

les ciseaux
à ongles
nail scissors

le coupe-
ongles
nail clippers

vocabulaire • vocabulary

le teint complexion	**sensible** sensitive	**antirides** antiwrinkle
clair fair	**hypoallergénique** hypoallergenic	**le beurre de cacao** cocoa butter
foncé dark	**le ton** shade	**les boules de coton** cotton balls
sec dry	**le bronzage** tan	
gras oily	**le tatouage** tattoo	

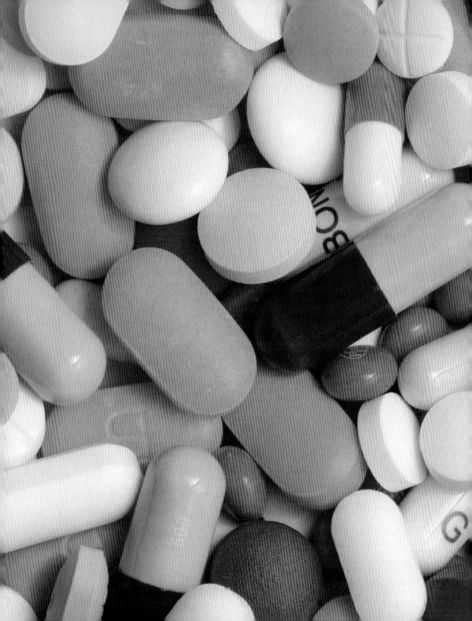

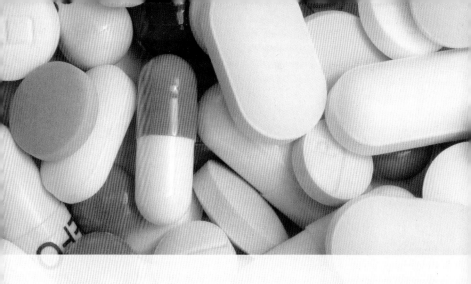

la santé
health

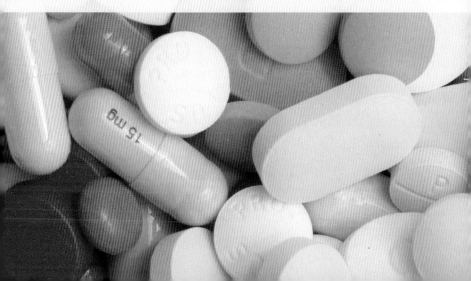

la maladie • illness

la fièvre | fever

l'inhalateur
inhaler

l'asthme
asthma

le mal de tête
headache

le saignement
de nez
nosebleed

la toux
cough

l'éternuement
sneeze

le rhume
cold

la grippe
flu

les maux de ventre
cramps

la nausée
nausea

la varicelle
chicken pox

l'éruption
cutanée
rash

---

vocabulaire • vocabulary

l'attaque stroke	le diabète diabetes	l'eczéma eczema	le coup de froid chill	vomir vomit (v)	la diarrhée diarrhea
la tension blood pressure	l'allergie allergy	l'infection infection	le mal d'estomac stomachache	l'épilepsie epilepsy	la rougeole measles
la crise cardiaque heart attack	le rhume des foins hay fever	le virus virus	s'évanouir faint (v)	la migraine migraine	les oreillons mumps

le médecin *m* / la médecin *f* • doctor

la consultation • consultation

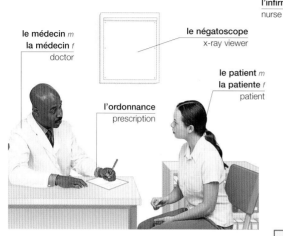

le médecin *m*
la médecin *f*
doctor

le négatoscope
x-ray viewer

l'ordonnance
prescription

le patient *m*
la patiente *f*
patient

l'infirmier *m*
l'infirmière *f*
nurse

la balance
scale

le brassard
cuff

le tensiomètre électronique
electric blood pressure monitor

---

vocabulaire • vocabulary

le rendez-vous appointment	**le thermomètre** thermometer
le cabinet doctor's office	**l'examen médical** medical examination
la salle d'attente waiting room	**la prothèse auditive** hearing aid
l'inoculation vaccination	

J'ai besoin de voir un médecin.
I need to see a doctor.

J'ai mal ici.
It hurts here.

la blessure • injury

l'écharpe
sling

la minerve
neck brace

la fracture
fracture

le coup du lapin
whiplash

l'entorse | sprain

la coupure
cut

l'écorchure
graze

la contusion
bruise

l'écharde
splinter

le coup de soleil
sunburn

la brûlure
burn

la morsure
bite

la piqûre
sting

---

vocabulaire • vocabulary

l'accident
accident

l'urgence
emergency

la blessure
wound

l'hémorragie
hemorrhage

l'ampoule
blister

l'empoisonnement
poisoning

le choc électrique
electric shock

le traumatisme crânien
head injury

la commotion cérébrale
concussion

Est-ce qu'il / elle va se remettre?
Will he / she be all right?

Où avez-vous mal?
Where does it hurt?

Appelez une ambulance s'il vous plaît.
Please call an ambulance.

les premiers secours • first aid

la pommade
ointment

le pansement
adhesive bandage

l'épingle de
sûreté
safety pin

le bandage
bandage

les analgésiques
painkillers

la lingette
antiseptique
antiseptic wipe

la pince à épiler
tweezers

les ciseaux
scissors

l'antiseptique
antiseptic

la trousse de premiers secours | first-aid kit

la gaze
gauze

le pansement
dressing

l'attelle
splint

le sparadrap
adhesive tape

la réanimation
resuscitation

vocabulaire • vocabulary			
le choc shock	le pouls pulse	étouffer choke (v)	**Est-ce que vous pouvez m'aider?** Can you help me?
sans connaissance unconscious	la respiration breathing	stérile sterile	**Pouvez-vous donner les soins d'urgence?** Do you know first aid?

l'hôpital • hospital

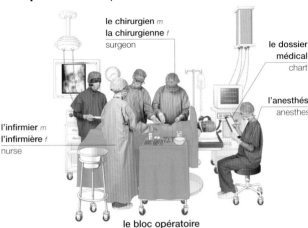

le chirurgien *m*
la chirurgienne *f*
surgeon

le dossier
médical
chart

l'infirmier *m*
l'infirmière *f*
nurse

l'anesthésiste *m/f*
anesthesiologist

le bloc opératoire
operating room

l'analyse de sang
blood test

l'injection
injection

le chariot
gurney

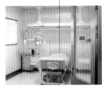

la salle des urgences
emergency room

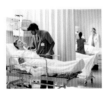

la salle
ward

le fauteuil roulant
wheelchair

la radio
x-ray

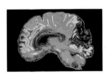

le scanner
scan

---

vocabulaire • vocabulary

l'opération operation	renvoyé *m* renvoyée *f* discharged	les heures de visite visiting hours	la pédiatrie children's ward	le service de soins intensifs intensive care unit
admis *m* admise *f* admitted	la clinique clinic	la maternité maternity ward	la chambre privée private room	le patient *m* / la patiente *f* en consultation externe outpatient

les services • departments

l'O.R.L.
ENT

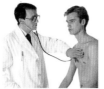

la cardiologie
cardiology

l'orthopédie
orthopedics

la gynécologie
gynecology

la kinésithérapie
physiotherapy

la dermatologie
dermatology

la pédiatrie
pediatrics

la radiologie
radiology

la chirurgie
surgery

la maternité
maternity

la psychiatrie
psychiatry

l'ophtalmologie
ophthalmology

---

vocabulaire • vocabulary

la neurologie neurology	l'urologie urology	l'endocrinologie endocrinology	la pathologie pathology	le résultat result
l'oncologie oncology	la chirurgie esthétique plastic surgery	l'orientation d'un patient referral	l'analyse test	le spécialiste *m* la spécialiste *f* specialist

---

le dentiste *m* / la dentiste *f* • dentist

la dent • tooth

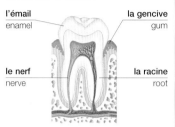

l'émail
enamel

la gencive
gum

le nerf
nerve

la racine
root

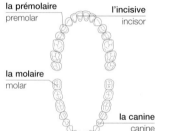

la prémolaire
premolar

l'incisive
incisor

la molaire
molar

la canine
canine

la visite de contrôle • checkup

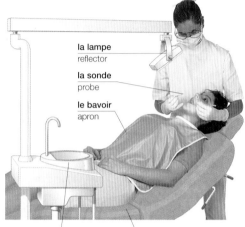

la lampe
reflector

la sonde
probe

le bavoir
apron

le crachoir
sink

le fauteuil de dentiste
dentist's chair

---

vocabulaire • vocabulary

la rage de dents
toothache

la plaque
plaque

la carie
decay

le plombage
filling

la facette
veneer

la brossette
interdentaire
interdental
brush

la fraise
drill

le fil dentaire
dental floss

l'extraction
extraction

la couronne
crown

utiliser le fil
dentaire
floss (v)

brosser
brush (v)

l'appareil
dentaire
braces

la radio dentaire
dental x-ray

la radio
x-ray film

le dentier
dentures

l'opticien *m* / l'opticienne *f* • optometrist

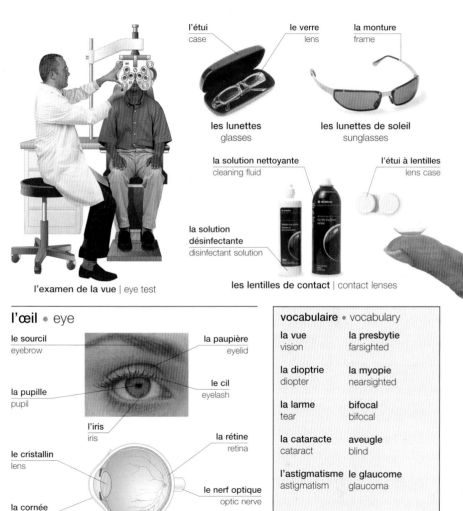

l'étui
case

le verre
lens

la monture
frame

les lunettes
glasses

les lunettes de soleil
sunglasses

la solution nettoyante
cleaning fluid

l'étui à lentilles
lens case

la solution
désinfectante
disinfectant solution

l'examen de la vue | eye test

les lentilles de contact | contact lenses

l'œil • eye

le sourcil
eyebrow

la paupière
eyelid

le cil
eyelash

la pupille
pupil

l'iris
iris

le cristallin
lens

la cornée
cornea

la rétine
retina

le nerf optique
optic nerve

vocabulaire • vocabulary	
la vue	la presbytie
vision	farsighted
la dioptrie	la myopie
diopter	nearsighted
la larme	bifocal
tear	bifocal
la cataracte	aveugle
cataract	blind
l'astigmatisme	le glaucome
astigmatism	glaucoma

la grossesse • pregnancy

le test de grossesse
pregnancy test

l'échographie
scan

le cordon
ombilical
umbilical cord

le placenta
placenta

le col de l'utérus
cervix

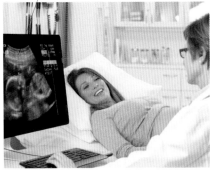

l'utérus
uterus

les ultrasons | ultrasound

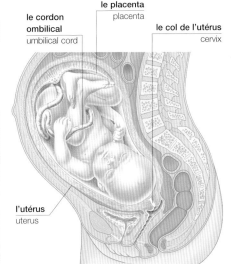

le fœtus | fetus

---

vocabulaire • vocabulary

l'ovulation ovulation	l'embryon embryo	le liquide amniotique amniotic fluid	l'accouchement delivery	donner le biberon bottle-feed (v)
la conception conception	l'utérus womb	la péridurale epidural	la fausse couche miscarriage	le gynécologue *m* la gynécologue *f* gynecologist
enceinte pregnant / expecting	le trimestre trimester	l'épisiotomie episiotomy	les points de suture stitches	l'obstétricien *m* l'obstétricienne *f* obstetrician
la naissance birth	l'amniocentèse amniocentesis	la césarienne cesarean section	l'accouchement par le siège breech birth	
prénatal *m* prénatale *f* prenatal	la contraction contraction la dilatation dilation	prématuré *m* prématurée *f* premature	le lait maternisé baby formula	J'ai perdu les eaux! My water broke!

---

la naissance • childbirth

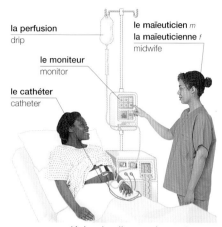

la perfusion
drip

le moniteur
monitor

le cathéter
catheter

le maïeuticien *m*
la maïeuticienne *f*
midwife

déclencher l'accouchement
induce labor (v)

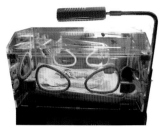

la couveuse | incubator

le poids de naissance
birth weight

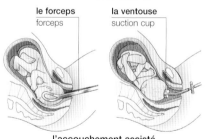

le forceps
forceps

la ventouse
suction cup

l'accouchement assisté
assisted delivery

le bracelet d'identité
identity tag

le nouveau-né *m/f*
newborn baby

l'allaitement • nursing

la pompe à lait
breast pump

**le soutien-gorge
d'allaitement**
nursing bra

donner le sein
breastfeed (v)

**les coussinets
d'allaitement**
nursing pads

les médecines complémentaires

complementary therapies

la posture de yoga
yoga pose

le tapis
mat

le yoga | yoga

le massage
massage

le shiatsu
shiatsu

la chiropractie
chiropractic

l'ostéopathie
osteopathy

la réflexologie
reflexology

la méditation
meditation

le thérapeute _m_
la thérapeute _f_
counselor

la thérapie de groupe
group therapy

le reiki
reiki

l'acuponcture
acupuncture

la médecine ayurvédique
ayurveda

l'hypnothérapie
hypnotherapy

les huiles essentielles
essential oils

l'herboristerie
herbalism

l'aromathérapie
aromatherapy

l'homéopathie
homeopathy

l'acupression
acupressure

le thérapeute _m_
la thérapeute _f_
therapist

la psychothérapie
psychotherapy

vocabulaire • vocabulary

l'hydrothérapie hydrotherapy	**la naturopathie** naturopathy	**la relaxation** relaxation	**la lithothérapie** crystal healing
le complément alimentaire supplement	**le feng shui** feng shui	**le stress** stress	**à base de plantes** herbal

la maison
home

la maison • house

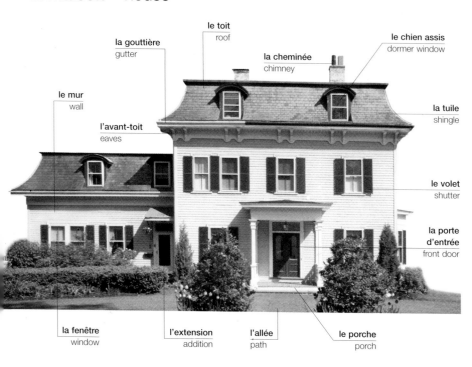

le toit
roof

la gouttière
gutter

la cheminée
chimney

le chien assis
dormer window

le mur
wall

l'avant-toit
eaves

la tuile
shingle

le volet
shutter

la porte
d'entrée
front door

la fenêtre
window

l'extension
addition

l'allée
path

le porche
porch

vocabulaire • vocabulary

individuelle single-family	**le pavillon** bungalow	**le grenier** attic	**la lampe d'entrée** porch light	**l'alarme** burglar alarm	**louer** rent (v)
mitoyenne duplex	**le sous-sol** basement	**la chambre** room	**le propriétaire** m **la propriétaire** f landlord	**la cour** courtyard	**le loyer** rent
la maison en rangée townhouse	**le garage** garage	**la boîte aux lettres** mailbox	**le locataire** m **la locataire** f tenant	**l'étage** floor	**attenante** row house

l'entrée • entrance

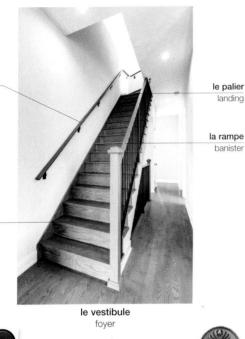

la main
courante
hand rail

le palier
landing

la rampe
banister

l'escalier
staircase

le vestibule
foyer

la sonnette
doorbell

le paillasson
doormat

le heurtoir
door knocker

la chaînette de sécurité
door chain

la clef
key

la serrure
lock

le verrou
bolt

l'appartement
apartment

le balcon
balcony

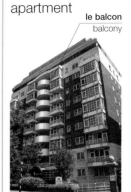

l'immeuble
apartment building

l'interphone
intercom

l'ascenseur
elevator

les systèmes domestiques • internal systems

la pale
blade

le ventilateur
fan

le radiateur
radiator

le chauffage d'appoint
space heater

le convecteur
convection heater

l'électricité • electricity

la prise de terre
ground pin

la broche
pin

neutre
neutral

sous tension
live

les fils
wires

l'ampoule basse consommation
energy-saving bulb

la fiche
plug

---

vocabulaire • vocabulary

la tension voltage	le fusible fuse	la prise de courant outlet	le courant continu direct current	la coupure de courant power outage
l'ampère amp	la boîte à fusibles fuse box	l'interrupteur switch	le transformateur transformer	le réseau électrique household current
le courant power	la génératrice generator	le courant alternatif alternating current	le compteur d'électricité electric meter	

la plomberie • plumbing

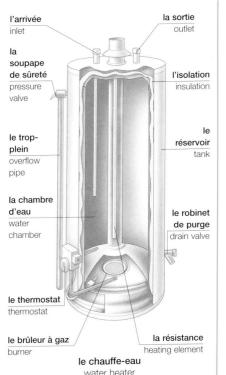

l'arrivée
inlet

la sortie
outlet

la soupape de sûreté
pressure valve

l'isolation
insulation

le trop-plein
overflow pipe

le réservoir
tank

la chambre d'eau
water chamber

le robinet de purge
drain valve

le thermostat
thermostat

le brûleur à gaz
burner

la résistance
heating element

le chauffe-eau
water heater

l'évier • sink

le robinet
faucet

la manette
lever

le joint
gasket

l'arrivée d'eau
supply pipe

le robinet de sectionnement
shut-off valve

le tuyau d'écoulement
drain

le broyeur d'ordures
waste disposal unit

les toilettes • toilet

la chasse-d'eau
tank

le flotteur
float ball

la lunette
seat

le tuyau d'écoulement
waste pipe

la cuvette
bowl

l'enlèvement de déchets • waste disposal

la bouteille
bottle

le couvercle
lid

la pédale
pedal

la poubelle à déchets recyclables
recycling bin

la poubelle
trash can

la poubelle à compartiments
sorting bin

les déchets organiques
organic waste

le salon • living room

l'applique
wall light

la cheminée
fireplace

le plafond
ceiling

le vase
vase

le coussin
pillow

la lampe
lamp

la table
basse
coffee table

le canapé
sofa

le sol
floor

le cadre
frame

l'image
picture

le rideau
curtain

le brise-bise
sheer curtain

le store vénitien
Venetian blinds

le store
roller blind

la moulure
molding

le fauteuil
armchair

la bibliothèque
bookshelf

le canapé-lit
sofa bed

le tapis
rug

le bureau | study

la salle à manger • dining room

le poivre
pepper

le sel
salt

la table
table

la
vaisselle
crockery

les couverts
cutlery

la chaise
chair

le dossier
back

le siège
seat

le pied
leg

vocabulaire • vocabulary

mettre la table set the table (v)	**(avoir) faim** hungry	**le petit déjeuner** breakfast	**rassasié** *m* **rassasiée** *f* full	**l'hôte** host	**Puis-je en reprendre un peu, s'il vous plaît?** Can I have some more, please?
servir serve (v)	**la nappe** tablecloth	**le déjeuner** lunch	**la portion** portion	**l'hôtesse** hostess	**Non merci, j'en ai eu assez.** I've had enough, thank you.
manger eat (v)	**le set de table** place mat	**le dîner** dinner	**le repas** meal	**l'invité** *m* **l'invitée** *f* guest	**C'était délicieux.** That was delicious.

la vaisselle et les couverts • crockery and cutlery

la cuiller à café
teaspoon

le mug
mug

la tasse à café
coffee cup

la tasse à thé
teacup

l'assiette
plate

le bol
bowl

la cafetière
French press

la théière
teapot

le pichet
pitcher

le coquetier
eggcup

le verre à vin
wine glass

le verre
tumbler

la verrerie
glassware

le rond de serviette
napkin ring

l'assiette à dessert
side plate

l'assiette plate
dinner plate

l'assiette creuse
soup bowl

la cuiller à soupe
soup spoon

la serviette
napkin

la fourchette
fork

le couvert
place setting

la cuiller
spoon

le couteau
knife

la cuisine • kitchen

la hotte
ventilation hood

la clayette
shelf

les plaques
de cuisson
céramique
ceramic
stovetop

la crédence
backsplash

le robinet
faucet

le plan de
travail
countertop

l'évier
sink

le four
oven

le tiroir
drawer

le placard
cabinet

les appareils ménagers • appliances

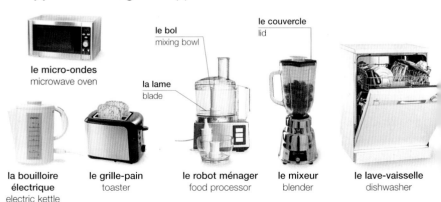

le micro-ondes
microwave oven

le bol
mixing bowl

le couvercle
lid

la lame
blade

la bouilloire
électrique
electric kettle

le grille-pain
toaster

le robot ménager
food processor

le mixeur
blender

le lave-vaisselle
dishwasher

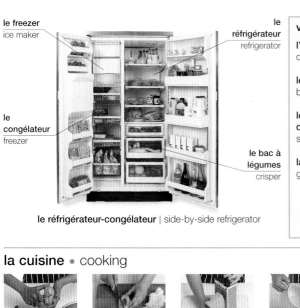

le freezer
ice maker

le réfrigérateur
refrigerator

le congélateur
freezer

le bac à légumes
crisper

le réfrigérateur-congélateur | side-by-side refrigerator

vocabulaire • vocabulary

l'égouttoir draining board	congeler freeze (v)
le brûleur burner	décongeler defrost (v)
les plaques de cuisson stovetop	cuire à la vapeur steam (v)
la poubelle garbage can	faire sauter sauté (v)

la cuisine • cooking

éplucher
peel (v)

couper
slice (v)

râper
grate (v)

verser
pour (v)

mélanger
mix (v)

battre
whisk (v)

bouillir
boil (v)

frire
fry (v)

étaler au rouleau
roll (v)

remuer
stir (v)

mijoter
simmer (v)

pocher
poach (v)

cuire au four
bake (v)

rôtir
roast (v)

griller
broil (v)

les ustensiles de cuisine • kitchenware

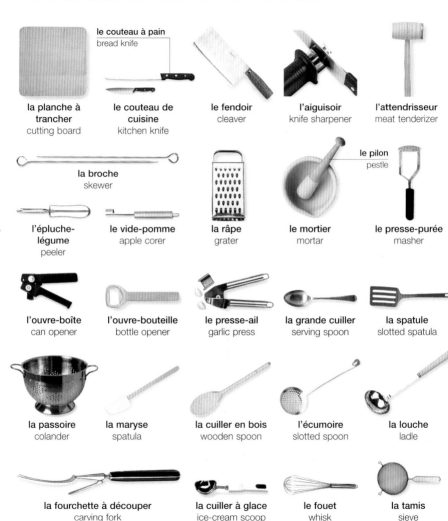

le couteau à pain
bread knife

la planche à trancher
cutting board

le couteau de cuisine
kitchen knife

le fendoir
cleaver

l'aiguisoir
knife sharpener

l'attendrisseur
meat tenderizer

la broche
skewer

le pilon
pestle

l'épluche-légume
peeler

le vide-pomme
apple corer

la râpe
grater

le mortier
mortar

le presse-purée
masher

l'ouvre-boîte
can opener

l'ouvre-bouteille
bottle opener

le presse-ail
garlic press

la grande cuiller
serving spoon

la spatule
slotted spatula

la passoire
colander

la maryse
spatula

la cuiller en bois
wooden spoon

l'écumoire
slotted spoon

la louche
ladle

la fourchette à découper
carving fork

la cuiller à glace
ice-cream scoop

le fouet
whisk

la tamis
sieve

le couvercle
lid

anti-adhérent
nonstick

la poêle
frying pan

la casserole
saucepan

le gril
grill pan

le wok
wok

le tajine
tagine

en verre
glass

allant au four
ovenproof

le saladier
mixing bowl

le moule à soufflé
soufflé dish

le plat à gratin
gratin dish

le ramequin
ramekin

la cocotte
casserole dish

la pâtisserie • baking cakes

la balance
scale

le verre mesureur
measuring cup

le moule à
gâteaux
cake pan

la tourtière
pie pan

le moule à tarte
quiche pan

le pinceau à pâtisserie
pastry brush

le rouleau à pâtisserie
rolling pin

la poche à douille
piping bag

le moule à
muffins
muffin pan

la plaque à
gâteaux
cookie sheet

la grille de
refroidissement
cooling rack

le gant isolant
oven mitt

le tablier
apron

la chambre • bedroom

l'armoire
closet

la lampe de chevet
bedside lamp

la tête de lit
headboard

la table de nuit
nightstand

la commode
chest of drawers

le tiroir
drawer

le lit
bed

le matelas
mattress

le couvre-lit
bedspread

l'oreiller
pillow

la bouillotte
hot-water bottle

le radio-réveil
clock radio

le réveil
alarm clock

la boîte de mouchoirs
box of tissues

le cintre
coat hanger

le linge de lit • bed linen

la taie d'oreiller
pillowcase

le drap
sheet

le miroir
mirror

la coiffeuse
dressing
table

la couette
comforter

l'édredon
quilt

**la
couverture**
blanket

le sol
floor

---

vocabulaire • vocabulary

le grand lit full bed	**le pied de lit** footboard	**l'insomnie** insomnia	**se réveiller** wake up (v)	**mettre le réveil** set the alarm (v)
le lit simple twin bed	**le sommier** bedspring	**se coucher** go to bed (v)	**se lever** get up (v)	**ronfler** snore (v)
la couverture chauffante electric blanket	**le tapis** carpet	**s'endormir** go to sleep (v)	**faire le lit** make the bed (v)	**l'armoire encastrée** closet

---

la salle de bain • bathroom

le porte-serviettes
towel rack

la porte de douche
shower door

le robinet d'eau froide
cold faucet

le robinet d'eau chaude
hot faucet

le pommeau de douche
shower head

le lavabo
sink

la bonde
plug

la douche
shower

l'évacuation
drain

la lunette des toilettes
toilet seat

les toilettes
toilet

la brosse
toilet brush

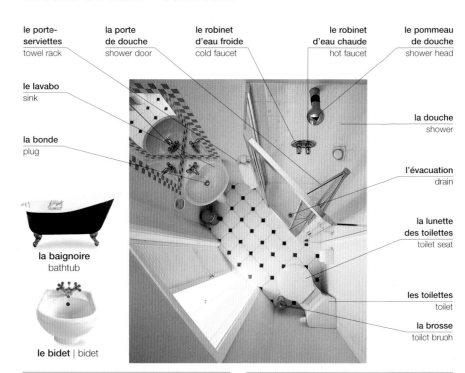

la baignoire
bathtub

le bidet | bidet

vocabulaire • vocabulary

l'armoire à pharmacie
medicine cabinet

le tapis de bain
bath mat

le rouleau de papier hygiénique
toilet paper

le rideau de douche
shower curtain

prendre une douche
take a shower (v)

prendre un bain
take a bath (v)

l'hygiène dentaire • dental hygiene

la brosse à dents
toothbrush

le fil dentaire
dental floss

le dentifrice
toothpaste

le bain de bouche
mouthwash

l'éponge
sponge

la pierre ponce
pumice stone

la brosse pour le dos
back brush

le déodorant
deodorant

le porte-savon
soap dish

le gel douche
shower gel

le savon
soap

la crème pour le visage
face cream

le bain moussant
bubble bath

la serviette
hand towel

**la serviette
de bain**
bath towel

les serviettes
towels

la lotion pour le corps
body lotion

le talc
talcum powder

le peignoir
bathrobe

le rasage • shaving

**le rasoir
électrique**
electric razor

la mousse à raser
shaving foam

le rasoir jetable
disposable razor

**la lame de
rasoir**
razor blade

l'after-shave
aftershave

la chambre d'enfants • nursery

les soins de bébé • baby care

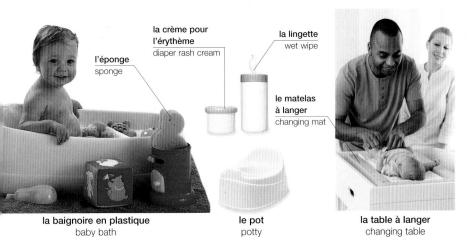

la crème pour l'érythème
diaper rash cream

la lingette
wet wipe

l'éponge
sponge

le matelas à langer
changing mat

la baignoire en plastique
baby bath

le pot
potty

la table à langer
changing table

le coucher • sleeping

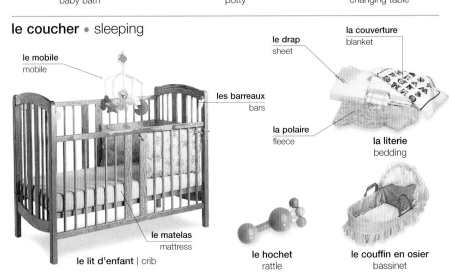

le mobile
mobile

le drap
sheet

la couverture
blanket

les barreaux
bars

la polaire
fleece

la literie
bedding

le matelas
mattress

le lit d'enfant | crib

le hochet
rattle

le couffin en osier
bassinet

le jeu • playing

la poupée
doll

la peluche
stuffed toy

la maison de poupée
dollhouse

la maison pliante
playhouse

la sécurité
safety

la sécurité enfant
child lock

le moniteur
baby monitor

l'ours en peluche
teddy bear

le jouet
toy

le panier à jouets
toy basket

la balle
ball

le parc
playpen

la barrière d'escalier
stair gate

l'alimentation
eating

la chaise haute
high chair

la tétine
nipple

le biberon
bottle

la tasse à bec
sippy cup

la sortie • going out

la poussette
stroller

la capote
hood

le landau
baby carriage

le couffin
carrier

la couche
diaper

le sac
diaper bag

le porte-bébé
baby sling

la buanderie • utility room

le linge • laundry

le linge sale
dirty laundry

le panier à linge
laundry basket

le lave-linge
washer

le lave-linge séchant
washer-dryer

le sèche-linge
dryer

la corde à linge
clothesline

le fer à repasser
iron

la pince à linge
clothespin

sécher
dry (v)

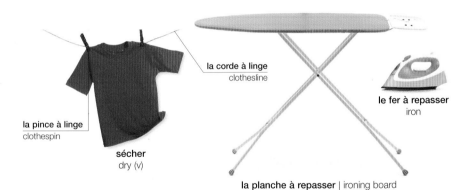

la planche à repasser | ironing board

---

vocabulaire • vocabulary

charger load (v)	**essorer** spin (v)	**repasser** iron (v)	**Comment fonctionne le lave-linge?** How do I operate the washing machine?
rincer rinse (v)	**l'essoreuse** spin-dryer	**l'assouplissant pour le linge** fabric softener	**Quel est le programme pour les couleurs / le blanc?** What is the setting for colors / whites?

l'équipement d'entretien • cleaning equipment

le tuyau flexible
suction hose

la balayette
brush

la pelle
dustpan

l'eau de Javel
bleach

le seau
bucket

le liquide
liquid

la poudre
powder

le chiffon
dust cloth

l'aspirateur
vacuum cleaner

la serpillière
mop

le détergent
detergent

la cire
polish

les activités • activities

nettoyer
clean (v)

laver
wash (v)

essuyer
wipe (v)

brosser
scrub (v)

racler
scrape (v)

le balai
broom

balayer
sweep (v)

épousseter
dust (v)

cirer
polish (v)

l'atelier • workshop

le mandrin
chuck

la mèche
drill bit

la batterie
battery pack

la scie sauteuse
jigsaw

la perceuse sans fil
cordless drill

la perceuse électrique
electric drill

le pistolet à colle
glue gun

le serre-joint
clamp

la lame
blade

l'étau
vise

la ponceuse
sander

la scie circulaire
circular saw

l'établi
workbench

la colle à bois
wood glue

le porte-outils
tool rack

la défonceuse
router

le vilebrequin
bit brace

les copeaux
wood shavings

la rallonge
extension cord

les techniques • techniques

découper
cut (v)

scier
saw (v)

percer
drill (v)

marteler
hammer (v)

raboter
plane (v)

tourner
turn (v)

sculpter
carve (v)

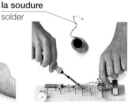
la soudure
solder

souder
solder (v)

les matériaux • materials

le médium
MDF

le contreplaqué
plywood

l'aggloméré
particle board

l'isorel
hardboard

le bois
tendre
softwood

le bois dur
hardwood

le vernis
varnish

la lasure
wood stain

le bois | wood

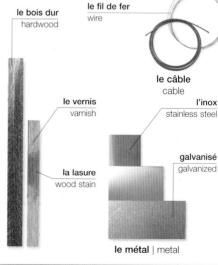

le fil de fer
wire

le câble
cable

l'inox
stainless steel

galvanisé
galvanized

le métal | metal

la boîte à outils • toolbox

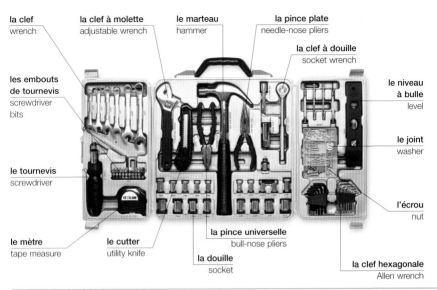

la clef
wrench

la clef à molette
adjustable wrench

le marteau
hammer

la pince plate
needle-nose pliers

la clef à douille
socket wrench

les embouts
de tournevis
screwdriver
bits

le niveau
à bulle
level

le joint
washer

le tournevis
screwdriver

l'écrou
nut

le mètre
tape measure

le cutter
utility knife

la pince universelle
bull-nose pliers

la douille
socket

la clef hexagonale
Allen wrench

les forets • drill bits

le foret à métaux
metal bit

le foret à bois plat
flat wood bit

l'alésoir
reamer

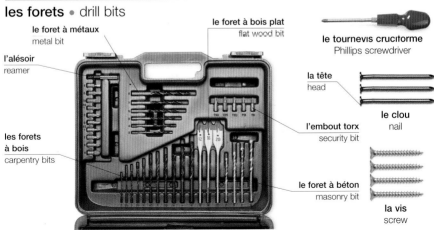

le tournevis cruciforme
Phillips screwdriver

la tête
head

l'embout torx
security bit

le clou
nail

les forets
à bois
carpentry bits

le foret à béton
masonry bit

la vis
screw

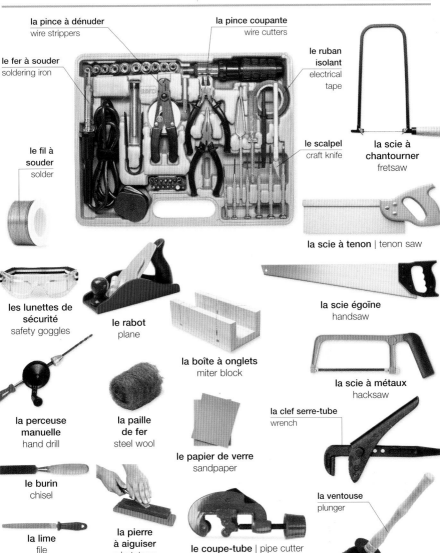

la pince à dénuder
wire strippers

la pince coupante
wire cutters

le fer à souder
soldering iron

le ruban
isolant
electrical
tape

le scalpel
craft knife

la scie à
chantourner
fretsaw

le fil à
souder
solder

la scie à tenon | tenon saw

les lunettes de
sécurité
safety goggles

le rabot
plane

la boîte à onglets
miter block

la scie égoïne
handsaw

la scie à métaux
hacksaw

la perceuse
manuelle
hand drill

la paille
de fer
steel wool

le papier de verre
sandpaper

la clef serre-tube
wrench

le burin
chisel

la ventouse
plunger

la lime
file

la pierre
à aiguiser
whetstone

le coupe-tube | pipe cutter

la décoration • decorating

les ciseaux
scissors

le peintre *m*
la peintre *f*
decorator

le cutter
utility knife

le papier peint
wallpaper

le fil à plomb
plumb line

le grattoir
putty knife

la brosse à tapisser
wallpaper brush

la table à encoller
pasting table

la brosse à encoller
pasting brush

la colle à tapisser
wallpaper paste

le seau
bucket

tapisser | wallpaper (v)

décoller
strip (v)

enduire
fill (v)

poncer
sand (v)

plâtrer | plaster (v)

poser | hang (v)

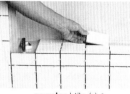

carreler | tile (v)

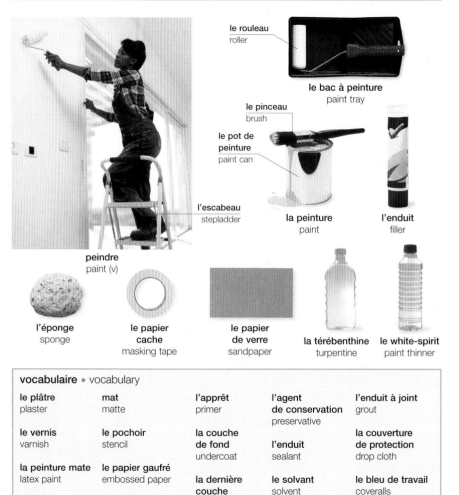

le rouleau
roller

le bac à peinture
paint tray

le pinceau
brush

le pot de peinture
paint can

l'escabeau
stepladder

la peinture
paint

l'enduit
filler

peindre
paint (v)

l'éponge
sponge

le papier cache
masking tape

le papier de verre
sandpaper

la térébenthine
turpentine

le white-spirit
paint thinner

vocabulaire • vocabulary

le plâtre plaster	mat matte	l'apprêt primer	l'agent de conservation preservative	l'enduit à joint grout
le vernis varnish	le pochoir stencil	la couche de fond undercoat	l'enduit sealant	la couverture de protection drop cloth
la peinture mate latex paint	le papier gaufré embossed paper	la dernière couche topcoat	le solvant solvent	le bleu de travail coveralls
brillant gloss	le papier d'apprêt lining paper			

le jardin • garden

les styles de jardin • garden styles

le patio
patio garden

le jardin à la française | formal garden

le jardin à l'anglaise
cottage garden

le jardin d'herbes aromatiques
herb garden

le jardin sur le toit
roof garden

le jardin de rocaille
rock garden

la cour
courtyard

le jardin d'eau
water garden

le panier suspendu
hanging basket

le treillis
trellis

la pergola
arbor

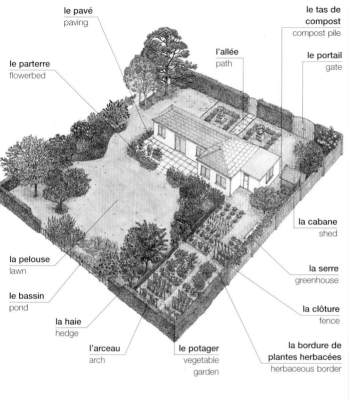

le pavé
paving

le parterre
flowerbed

l'allée
path

le tas de
compost
compost pile

le portail
gate

le sol • soil

la pelouse
lawn

le bassin
pond

la haie
hedge

l'arceau
arch

le potager
vegetable
garden

la cabane
shed

la serre
greenhouse

la clôture
fence

la bordure de
plantes herbacées
herbaceous border

la terre
topsoil

le sol sableux
sand

le sol calcaire
chalk

le sol limoneux
silt

le sol argileux
clay

les planches
deck

la fontaine | fountain

les plantes de jardin • garden plants

les genres de plantes • types of plants

annuel
annual

bisannuel
biennial

vivace
perennial

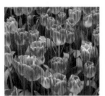

le bulbe
bulb

la fougère
fern

le jonc
cattail

le bambou
bamboo

les mauvaises herbes
weeds

l'herbe aromatique
herb

la plante aquatique
water plant

l'arbre
tree

le palmier
palm

le conifère
conifer

à feuilles persistantes
evergreen

à feuilles caduques
deciduous

la topiaire
topiary

la plante alpestre
alpine

la plante grasse
succulent

le cactus
cactus

la plante en pot
potted plant

la plante d'ombre
shade plant

la plante
grimpante
climber

l'arbuste
à fleurs
flowering shrub

la couverture
végétale
ground cover

la plante rampante
creeper

ornemental
ornamental

l'herbe
grass

les outils de jardin • garden tools

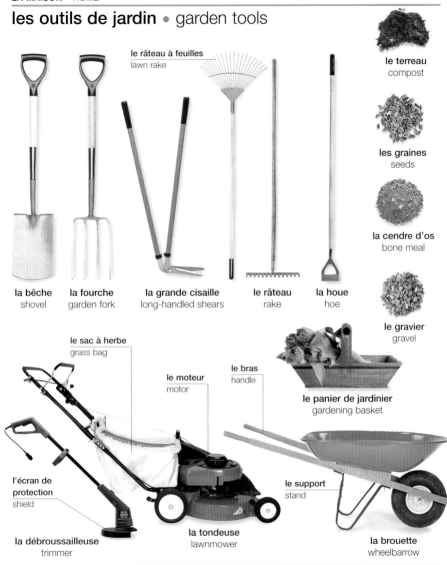

le râteau à feuilles
lawn rake

le terreau
compost

les graines
seeds

la cendre d'os
bone meal

la bêche
shovel

la fourche
garden fork

la grande cisaille
long-handled shears

le râteau
rake

la houe
hoe

le gravier
gravel

le sac à herbe
grass bag

le moteur
motor

le bras
handle

le panier de jardinier
gardening basket

l'écran de protection
shield

le support
stand

la débroussailleuse
trimmer

la tondeuse
lawnmower

la brouette
wheelbarrow

la petite fourche
hand fork

le déplantoir
trowel

la lame
blade

la cisaille
shears

la scie à main
handsaw

le sécateur
pruners

le germoir
seed tray

le pesticide
pesticide

le tamis
sieve

les gants de jardinage
gardening gloves

la ficelle
twine

les étiquettes
labels

les liens torsadés
twist ties

les anneaux
ring ties

les tuteurs
canes

le pot à fleurs
plant pot

les bottes
rubber boots

l'arrosage • watering

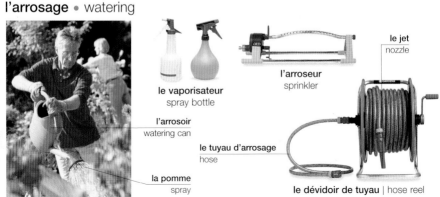

le vaporisateur
spray bottle

l'arrosoir
watering can

la pomme
spray

l'arroseur
sprinkler

le jet
nozzle

le tuyau d'arrosage
hose

le dévidoir de tuyau | hose reel

le jardinage • gardening

la pelouse
lawn

la haie
hedge

le parterre
flowerbed

la tondeuse
lawnmower

le tuteur
stake

tondre | mow (v)

gazonner
sod (v)

piquer
spike (v)

ratisser
rake (v)

tailler
trim (v)

bêcher
dig (v)

semer
sow (v)

fertiliser
top dress (v)

arroser
water (v)

le tuteur
cane

palisser
train (v)

enlever les fleurs fanées
deadhead (v)

asperger
spray (v)

greffer
graft (v)

la bouture
cutting
bouturer
propagate (v)

élaguer
prune (v)

mettre un tuteur
stake (v)

transplanter
transplant (v)

désherber
weed (v)

pailler
mulch (v)

récolter
harvest (v)

vocabulaire • vocabulary

cultiver cultivate (v)	**aménager** landscape (v)	**fertiliser** fertilize (v)	**tamiser** sift (v)	**organique** *m/f* organic	**le semis** seedling	**le sous-sol** subsoil
soigner tend (v)	**mettre en pot** pot (v)	**cueillir** pick (v)	**retourner** aerate (v)	**le drainage** drainage	**l'engrais** fertilizer	**l'herbicide** weedkiller

les services
services

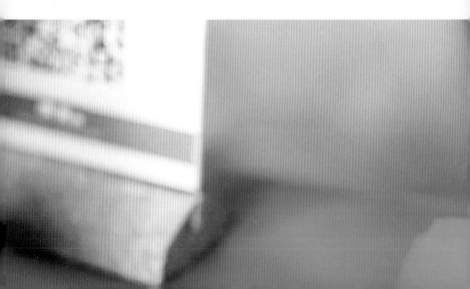

les services d'urgence • emergency services

l'ambulance • ambulance

l'ambulance
ambulance

le brancard
stretcher

le secouriste *m* / la secouriste *f*
paramedic

la police • police

le badge
badge

l'uniforme
uniform

le pistolet
gun

la matraque
nightstick

les menottes
handcuffs

le policier *m* / la policière *f*
police officer

les feux
lights

la sirène
siren

la voiture de police
police car

le poste de police
police station

vocabulaire • vocabulary

l'inspecteur *m* l'inspectrice *f* captain	le cambriolage burglary	l'empreinte fingerprint	l'arrestation arrest
le détective *m* la détective *f* detective	le suspect *m* la suspecte *f* suspect	l'agression assault	la cellule cell
l'acte répréhensible crime	l'enquête investigation	la plainte complaint	l'accusation charge

les pompiers • fire department

le casque
helmet

la fumée
smoke

la lance
hose

la nacelle
basket

les sapeurs-pompiers *m*
les sapeuses-pompières *f*
firefighters

le jet d'eau
water jet

la flèche
boom

l'incendie | fire

l'échelle
ladder

la cabine
cab

la caserne de pompiers
fire station

l'escalier de secours
fire escape

le camion de pompiers
fire engine

le détecteur
de fumée
smoke alarm

l'alarme
incendie
fire alarm

la hache
ax

l'extincteur
fire extinguisher

la borne
d'incendie
hydrant

La police / les pompiers / une ambulance, s'il vous plaît. I need the police / fire department / an ambulance.	Il y a un incendie à… There's a fire at…	Il y a eu un accident. There's been an accident.	Appelez la police! Call the police!

la banque • bank

la vitre
window

le guichetier *m*
la guichetière *f*
teller

le client *m*
la cliente *f*
customer

le guichet
counter

la carte de débit
debit card

le numéro
de compte
account number

le montant
amount

le lecteur
de cartes
card reader

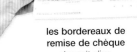

la carte de débit
debit card

la carte de crédit
credit card

les bordereaux de
remise de chèque
deposit slips

---

vocabulaire • vocabulary

l'épargne savings	le prêt immobilier mortgage	le paiement payment	verser deposit (v)	le compte courant checking account
l'impôt tax	le découvert overdraft	le prélèvement automatic payment	les frais bancaires bank charge	le compte d'épargne savings account
le prêt loan	le taux d'intérêt interest rate	la fiche de retrait withdrawal slip	le virement bancaire bank transfer	le code secret PIN

---

français • english

l'application
bancaire
banking app

la banque en ligne
online banking

la pièce
coin

le billet
bill

l'argent
money

l'écran
screen

le clavier
keypad

la fente
card reader

le distributeur
ATM

les devises étrangères
foreign currency

le bureau de change
currency exchange

le taux de change
exchange rate

la finance • finance

le conseiller financier m
la conseillère financière f
financial advisor

**le prix
des actions**
share price

le courtier m
la courtière f
stockbroker

la bourse
stock exchange

vocabulaire • vocabulary

encaisser
cash (v)

la valeur
denomination

la commission
commission

l'investissement
investment

les titres
stocks

la cybermonnaie
digital currency

les actions
shares

les dividendes
dividends

le portefeuille
portfolio

l'action
equity

le comptable m
la comptable f
accountant

**Est-ce que je peux changer ça,
s'il vous plaît?**
Can I change this, please?

**Quel est le taux de change
aujourd'hui?**
What's today's exchange rate?

les communications • communications

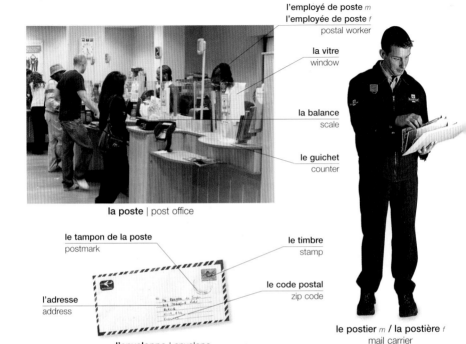

l'employé de poste *m*
l'employée de poste *f*
postal worker

la vitre
window

la balance
scale

le guichet
counter

la poste | post office

le tampon de la poste
postmark

le timbre
stamp

le code postal
zip code

l'adresse
address

l'enveloppe | envelope

le postier *m* / la postière *f*
mail carrier

---

vocabulaire • vocabulary

la lettre letter	**l'expéditeur** return address	**la distribution** delivery	**le sac postal** mailbag
par avion by airmail	**la signature** signature	**le tarif d'affran-chissement** postage	**ne pas plier** do not bend (v)
l'envoi en recommandé registered mail	**la levée** pickup	**fragile** fragile	**dessus** this way up

la boîte aux lettres
mailbox

la boîte aux lettres
letter slot

le colis
package

le coursier *m*
la coursière *f*
courier

le téléphone • telephone

le combiné
handset

le répondeur
answering machine

la base
base station

le clavier
keypad

le téléphone sans fil
cordless phone

l'appli
app

le smartphone
smartphone

vocabulaire • vocabulary

le wifi Wi-Fi	**le message vocal** voice message	**le portable** cell phone	**Pouvez-vous me donner le numéro de... ?** Can you give me the number for... ?	**Envoie-moi un SMS!** Text me!
composer dial (v)	**occupé** busy	**les données mobiles** mobile data		
répondre answer (v)	**coupé** disconnected	**l'itinérance des données** data roaming	**Quel est l'indicatif pour... ?** What is the area code for... ?	
le SMS text (SMS)	**le mot de passe** passcode			

l'hôtel • hotel

le hall • lobby

la carte-clé
key card

le client *m*
la cliente *f*
guest

le réceptionniste *m*
la réceptionniste *f*
receptionist

le comptoir
counter

la réception | reception

les bagages
luggage

le diable
cart

le bagagiste *m* / la bagagiste *f*
porter

l'ascenseur
elevator

le numéro de chambre
room number

les chambres • rooms

la chambre simple
single room

la chambre double
double room

la chambre à deux lits
twin room

la salle de bain privée
private bathroom

les services • services

le service de ménage
maid service

le service de blanchisserie
laundry service

le plateau à petit déjeuner
breakfast tray

le service d'étage | room service

le minibar
minibar

le restaurant
restaurant

la salle de sport
gym

la piscine
swimming pool

---

vocabulaire • vocabulary

la chambre avec le petit déjeuner
bed and breakfast

la pension complète
all meals included

la demi-pension
some meals included

Avez-vous une chambre de libre?
Do you have any vacancies?

J'ai une réservation.
I have a reservation.

Je voudrais une chambre simple.
I'd like a single room.

Je voudrais une chambre pour trois nuits.
I'd like a room for three nights.

C'est combien par nuit?
What is the charge per night?

Quand est-ce que je dois quitter la chambre?
When do I have to check out?

les courses
shopping

le centre commercial • shopping center

l'atrium
atrium

le deuxième
étage
third floor

le premier
étage
second floor

le client *m*
la cliente *f*
customer

l'escalier
mécanique
escalator

le rez-de-
chaussée
ground floor

vocabulaire • vocabulary

le rayon enfants
children's department

le rayon bagages
luggage department

le rayon chaussures
shoe department

le guide
store directory

**l'assistant
commercial** *m*
**l'assistante
commerciale** *f*
salesclerk

**le service
après-vente**
customer services

les cabines d'essayage
fitting rooms

les soins de bébés
baby changing room

les toilettes
restroom

C'est combien?
How much is this?

**Est-ce que je peux
changer ça?**
May I exchange this?

le grand magasin • department store

les vêtements pour hommes
menswear

les vêtements pour femmes
womens wear

la lingerie
lingerie

la parfumerie
perfumes

la beauté
cosmetics

le linge de maison
linens

l'ameublement
home furnishings

la mercerie
notions

la vaisselle
kitchenware

la porcelaine
china

l'électroménager
electronics

l'éclairage
lighting

les articles de sport
sportswear

les jouets
toys

la papeterie
stationery

l'alimentation
groceries

le supermarché • supermarket

le client *m*
la cliente *f*
customer

le caissier *m*
la caissière *f*
checker

le rayon
aisle

le rayonnage
shelf

les promotions
specials

la caisse | checkout

le sac à provisions
shopping bag

la caisse
cash register

le tapis roulant
conveyor belt

les provisions
groceries

l'anse
handle

780863 185779

le code barres
bar code

le caddie
grocery cart

le panier
basket

le lecteur optique
scanner

la boulangerie
bakery

les produits laitiers
dairy

les céréales
breakfast cereals

les conserves
canned food

la confiserie
candy

les légumes
vegetables

les fruits
fruit

la viande et la volaille
meat and poultry

le poisson
fish

la charcuterie
deli

les produits surgelés
frozen food

les plats cuisinés
prepared food

les boissons
drinks

les produits d'entretien
household products

les articles de toilette
toiletries

les articles pour bébés
baby products

l'électroménager
electrical goods

la nourriture pour animaux
pet food

les magazines | magazines

la pharmacie · drugstore

les soins
dentaires
dental care

l'hygiène
féminine
feminine
hygiene

les déodorants
deodorants

les vitamines
vitamins

l'officine
pharmacy

le pharmacien *m*
la pharmacienne *f*
pharmacist

le médicament
pour la toux
cough medicine

les remèdes à
base de plantes
herbal remedies

les soins de la peau
skin care

l'après-soleil
aftersun lotion

l'écran solaire
sunscreen

l'écran total
sunblock

le répulsif
insect repellent

la lingette humide
wet wipe

le mouchoir
tissue

la serviette hygiénique
sanitary napkin

le tampon
tampon

le protège-slip
panty liner

la gélule
capsule

la cuiller
pour mesurer
measuring spoon

le comprimé
pill

le sirop
syrup

la notice
instructions

l'inhalateur
inhaler

la crème
cream

la pommade
ointment

le gel
gel

le suppositoire
suppository

le compte-
gouttes
dropper

les gouttes
drops

l'aiguille
needle

la seringue
syringe

le spray
spray

la poudre
powder

---

vocabulaire • vocabulary

le fer iron	**les effets** **secondaires** side effects	**soluble** *m/f* soluble	**le masque** face mask	**l'anti-** **inflammatoire** anti-inflammatory
le calcium calcium	**la date d'expiration** expiration date	**la posologie** dosage	**la pastille pour** **la gorge** throat lozenge	**le médicament** **contre la diarrhée** diarrhea
le magnésium magnesium	**les comprimés** **contre le mal** **des transports** motion-sickness pills	**le traitement** medication **le médicament** medicine	**l'analgésique** painkiller **le sédatif** sedative	medication
l'insuline insulin				
le multivitamines multivitamins	**jetable** disposable	**le laxatif** laxative	**le somnifère** sleeping pill	

le magasin de fleurs • florist

les fleurs
flowers

le lis
lily

l'acacia
acacia

l'œillet
carnation

**la plante
en pot**
potted plant

le glaïeul
gladiolus

l'iris
iris

la marguerite
daisy

**le
chrysanthème**
chrysanthemum

la gypsophile
baby's breath

la giroflée	**le gerbera**	**le feuillage**	**la rose**	**le freesia**
stock	gerbera	foliage	rose	freesia

le vase
vase

l'orchidée
orchid

la pivoine
peony

la botte
bunch

la tige
stem

la jonquille
daffodil

le bouton
bud

l'emballage
wrapping

la tulipe | tulip

les compositions florales • arrangements

le ruban
ribbon

le bouquet
bouquet

les fleurs séchées
dried flowers

le pot-pourri | potpourri

la couronne | wreath

la guirlande
de fleurs
garland

vocabulaire • vocabulary

Je peux y attacher un message?
Can I attach a message?

Est-ce qu'elles sentent bon?
Are they fragrant?

Pouvez-vous les emballer?
Can I have them wrapped?

Elles tiennent combien de temps?
How long will these last?

Pouvez-vous les envoyer à… ?
Can you send them to… ?

Je voudrais un bouquet de…, s'il vous plaît.
Can I have a bunch of…, please?

le marchand de journaux • newsstand

le paquet de
cigarettes
pack of cigarettes

le briquet
lighter

le cendrier
ashtray

les timbres
stamps

la carte postale
postcard

la bande dessinée
comic book

le magazine
magazine

le journal
newspaper

fumer • smoking

le tabac
tobacco

le cigare
cigar

la cigarette électronique
vape

l'e-liquide
vape liquid

la confiserie • candy store

la boîte de chocolats	la barre chocolatée	les chips
box of chocolates	snack bar	potato chips

vocabulaire • vocabulary

le chocolat au lait milk chocolate	**le caramel** caramel
le chocolat noir dark chocolate	**la truffe** truffle
le chocolat blanc white chocolate	**le biscuit** cookie
les bonbons assortis pick and mix	**les bonbons durs** boiled sweets

la confiserie • confectionery

le chocolat
chocolate

la tablette de chocolat
chocolate bar

les bonbons
hard candy

la sucette
lollipop

le caramel
toffee

le nougat
nougat

la guimauve
marshmallow

le bonbon à la menthe
mint

le chewing-gum
chewing gum

la dragée à la gelée
jellybean

le bonbon au fruit
gumdrop

le réglisse
licorice

les autres magasins • other stores

la boulangerie
bakery

la pâtisserie
pastry shop

la boucherie
butcher shop

la poissonnerie
fish counter

le primeur
produce stand

l'épicerie
grocery store

**le magasin de
chaussures**
shoe store

la quincaillerie
hardware store

**le magasin
d'antiquités**
antiques store

**la boutique de
cadeaux**
gift shop

l'agence de voyage
travel agency

la bijouterie
jewelry store

la librairie
bookstore

**le magasin de
vins et spiritueux**
liquor store

l'animalerie
pet supplies store

**le magasin
de meubles**
furniture store

la boutique
boutique

vocabulaire • vocabulary

l'agent immobilier
real estate office

la pépinière
garden center

le pressing
dry cleaner

**la laverie
automatique**
laundromat

la serrurerie
locksmith

la charcuterie
deli

**le magasin de
produits diététiques**
health food store

**le magasin
d'occasion**
secondhand store

la boutique d'art
art supply store

le tailleur
tailor shop

le salon de coiffure
salon

**le magasin
de téléphonie**
phone store

la cordonnerie
shoe repairs

le marché | market

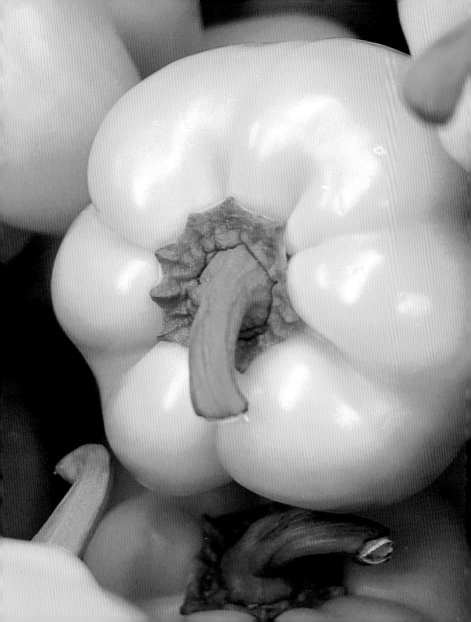

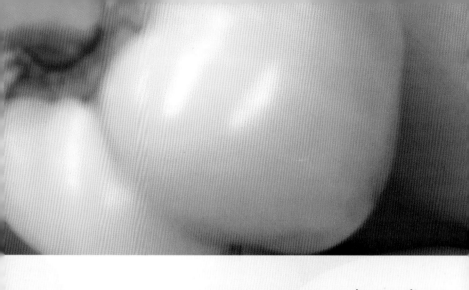

la nourriture
food

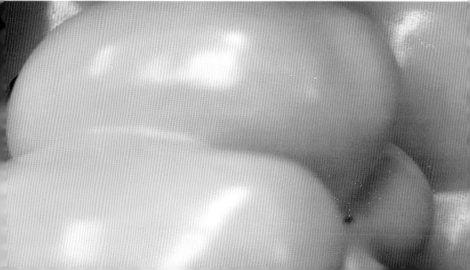

la viande • meat

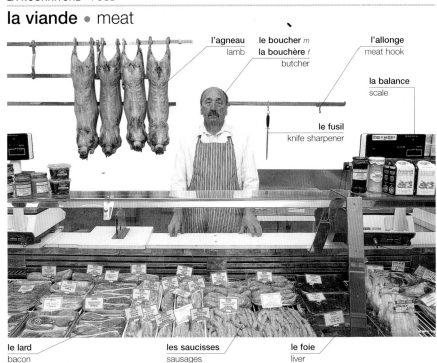

l'agneau
lamb

le boucher *m*
la bouchère *f*
butcher

l'allonge
meat hook

la balance
scale

le fusil
knife sharpener

le lard
bacon

les saucisses
sausages

le foie
liver

vocabulaire • vocabulary

le porc	la chèvre	la langue de bœuf	de ferme	la viande rouge
pork	goat	tongue	free-range	red meat
le bœuf	le lapin	les abats	le gibier à plume	la viande maigre
beef	rabbit	variety meat	game	lean meat
le veau	casher	fumé *m* / fumée *f*	bio / biologique *m/f*	la viande cuite
veal	kosher	smoked	organic	cooked meat
la venaison	halal	séché *m* / séchée *f*	la viande blanche	
venison	halal	cured	white meat	

les morceaux de viande • cuts

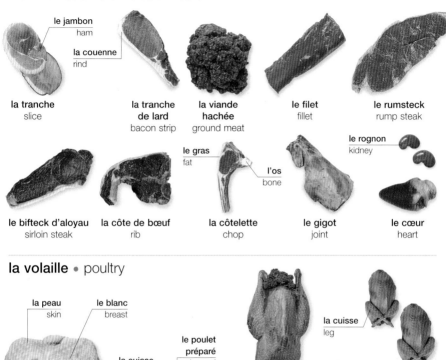

le jambon
ham

la couenne
rind

la tranche
slice

la tranche de lard
bacon strip

la viande hachée
ground meat

le filet
fillet

le rumsteck
rump steak

le gras
fat

l'os
bone

le rognon
kidney

le bifteck d'aloyau
sirloin steak

la côte de bœuf
rib

la côtelette
chop

le gigot
joint

le cœur
heart

la volaille • poultry

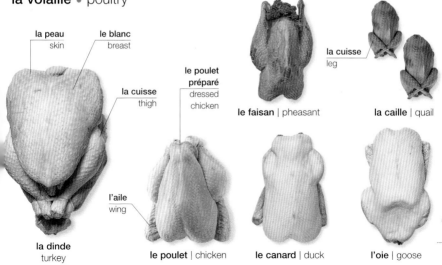

la peau
skin

le blanc
breast

la cuisse
thigh

le poulet préparé
dressed chicken

le faisan | pheasant

la cuisse
leg

la caille | quail

l'aile
wing

la dinde
turkey

le poulet | chicken

le canard | duck

l'oie | goose

le poisson • fish

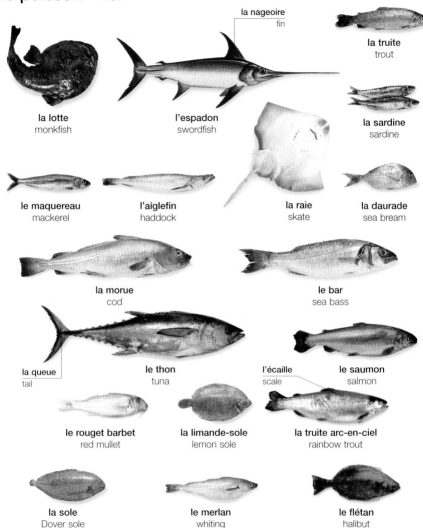

la nageoire
fin

la truite
trout

la lotte
monkfish

l'espadon
swordfish

la sardine
sardine

le maquereau
mackerel

l'aiglefin
haddock

la raie
skate

la daurade
sea bream

la morue
cod

le bar
sea bass

la queue
tail

le thon
tuna

l'écaille
scale

le saumon
salmon

le rouget barbet
red mullet

la limande-sole
lemon sole

la truite arc-en-ciel
rainbow trout

la sole
Dover sole

le merlan
whiting

le flétan
halibut

les fruits de mer • seafood

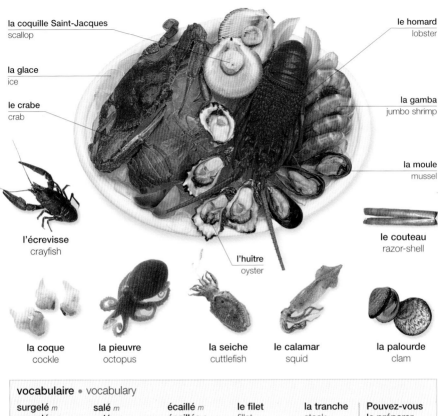

la coquille Saint-Jacques
scallop

le homard
lobster

la glace
ice

le crabe
crab

la gamba
jumbo shrimp

la moule
mussel

l'écrevisse
crayfish

le couteau
razor-shell

l'huître
oyster

la coque
cockle

la pieuvre
octopus

la seiche
cuttlefish

le calamar
squid

la palourde
clam

---

vocabulaire • vocabulary

surgelé *m* **surgelée** *f* frozen	**salé** *m* **salée** *f* salted	**écaillé** *m* **écaillée** *f* scaled	**le filet** fillet	**la tranche** steak	**Pouvez-vous le préparer pour moi?** Will you clean it for me?
frais *m* **fraîche** *f* fresh	**fumé** *m* **fumée** *f* smoked	**sans arêtes** boned	**en filets** filleted	**l'arête** bone	
nettoyé *m* **nettoyée** *f* cleaned	**sans peau** skinned	**la crevette** shrimp	**la longe** loin		

les légumes • vegetables (1)

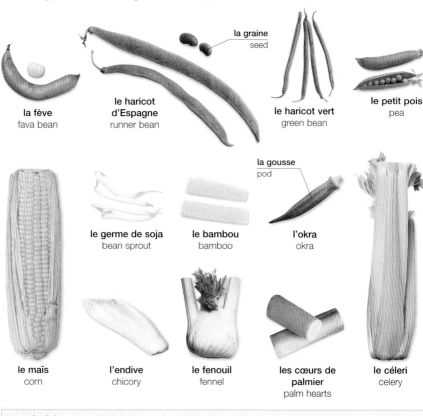

la graine
seed

la fève
fava bean

**le haricot
d'Espagne**
runner bean

le haricot vert
green bean

le petit pois
pea

la gousse
pod

le germe de soja
bean sprout

le bambou
bamboo

l'okra
okra

le maïs
corn

l'endive
chicory

le fenouil
fennel

**les cœurs de
palmier**
palm hearts

le céleri
celery

---

vocabulaire • vocabulary

la feuille leaf	**la fleurette** floret	**la pointe** tip	**bio / biologique** *m/f* organic	**Est-ce que vous vendez des légumes bios?** Do you sell organic vegetables?
la tige stalk	**le grain** kernel	**le cœur** heart	**le sac en plastique** plastic bag	**Est-ce qu'ils sont cultivés dans la région?** Are these grown locally?

---

la roquette
arugula

le cresson
watercress

la salade Trévise
radicchio

le chou de Bruxelles
Brussels sprouts

la bette
Swiss chard

le chou frisé
kale

l'oseille
sorrel

la chicorée
endive

le pissenlit
dandelion

les épinards
spinach

le chou-rave
kohlrabi

le chou chinois
bok choy

la laitue
lettuce

le brocoli
broccoli

le chou
cabbage

le chou précoce
spring greens

les légumes • vegetables (2)

le navet
turnip

l'artichaut
artichoke

le radis
radish

le chou-fleur
cauliflower

l'asperge
asparagus

la pomme
de terre
potato

la courge
squash

l'oignon
onion

le poivron
bell pepper

le piment
chili pepper

le maïs
corn

---

vocabulaire • vocabulary

la tomate cerise cherry tomato	**le taro** taro root	**cru** *m* **crue** *f* raw	**ferme** *m/f* firm	**Puis-je avoir un kilo de pommes de terre, s'il vous plaît?** Can I have one kilo of potatoes, please?
la carotte carrot	**le manioc** cassava	**piquant** *m* **piquante** *f* hot (spicy)	**la pulpe** flesh	
le fruit à pain breadfruit	**la châtaigne d'eau** water chestnut	**sucré** *m* **sucrée** *f* sweet	**la racine** root	**C'est combien le kilo?** What's the price per kilo?
la pomme de terre nouvelle new potato	**surgelé** *m* **surgelée** *f* frozen	**amer** *m* **amère** *f* bitter		**Ils s'appellent comment?** What are those called?
le céleri-rave celeriac				

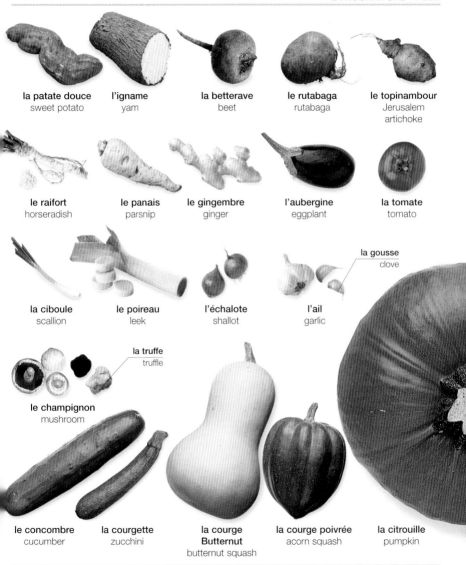

la patate douce
sweet potato

l'igname
yam

la betterave
beet

le rutabaga
rutabaga

le topinambour
Jerusalem
artichoke

le raifort
horseradish

le panais
parsnip

le gingembre
ginger

l'aubergine
eggplant

la tomate
tomato

la gousse
clove

la ciboule
scallion

le poireau
leek

l'échalote
shallot

l'ail
garlic

la truffe
truffle

le champignon
mushroom

le concombre
cucumber

la courgette
zucchini

la courge
Butternut
butternut squash

la courge poivrée
acorn squash

la citrouille
pumpkin

les fruits • fruit (1)

les agrumes • citrus fruit

l'orange
orange

la clémentine
clementine

la peau
blanche
pith

le tangelo
ugli fruit

le pamplemousse
grapefruit

le quartier
segment

la satsuma
satsuma

la mandarine
tangerine

le zeste
zest

le citron vert
lime

le citron
lemon

le kumquat
kumquat

les fruits à noyau • stone fruit

la pêche
peach

la nectarine
nectarine

l'abricot
apricot

la prune
plum

la cerise
cherry

la pomme
apple

la poire
pear

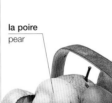

la corbeille de fruits | basket of fruit

les fruits rouges et les melons • berries and melons

la fraise
strawberry

la framboise
raspberry

la mûre
blackberry

la groseille
red currant

le cassis
black currant

le melon
melon

les raisins
grapes

la canneberge
cranberry

la myrtille
blueberry

la loganberry
loganberry

la groseille blanche
white currant

l'écorce
rind

le pépin
seed

la chair
flesh

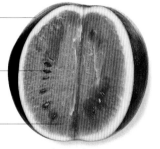
la pastèque
watermelon

la groseille à maquereau
gooseberry

vocabulaire • vocabulary

la rhubarbe rhubarb	**frais** *m* **fraîche** *f* fresh	**pourri** *m* **pourrie** *f* rotten	**sans pépins** seedless	**Est-ce qu'ils sont mûrs?** Are they ripe?
le fibre fiber	**juteux** *m* **juteuse** *f* juicy	**la pulpe** pulp		**Je peux goûter?** Can I try one?
sucré *m* **sucrée** *f* sweet	**croquant** *m* **croquante** *f* crisp	**le jus** juice		**Ils se gardent combien de temps?** How long will they keep?
acide *m/f* sour		**le trognon** core		

les fruits • fruit (2)

la mangue
mango

l'avocat
avocado

la pêche
peach

le kiwi
kiwifruit

l'ananas
pineapple

la papaye
papaya

le litchi
lychee

le physalis
cape gooseberry

le pépin
seed

la peau
peel

le coing
quince

le fruit de la passion
passion fruit

la banane
banana

la goyave
guava

la grenade
pomegranate

le kaki
persimmon

le feijoa
feijoa

la figue de Barbarie
prickly pear

la carambole
starfruit

le tamarillo
tamarillo

les noix et les fruits secs • nuts and dried fruit

le pignon
pine nut

la pistache
pistachio

la noix de cajou
cashew

la cacahouète
peanut

la noisette
hazelnut

la noix du Brésil
Brazil nut

la noix de pécan
pecan

l'amande
almond

la noix
walnut

le marron
chestnut

la noix de Macadamia
macadamia

la figue
fig

la datte
date

le pruneau
prune

la coquille
shell

la chair
flesh

le raisin de Smyrne
sultana

le raisin sec
raisin

le raisin de Corinthe
currant

la noix de coco
coconut

vocabulaire • vocabulary

vert *m*	dur *m*	le noyau	salé *m*	grillé *m*	décortiqué *m*	le fruit confit
verte *f*	dure *f*	kernel	salée *f*	grillée *f*	décortiquée *f*	candied fruit
green	hard		salted	roasted	shelled	
		séché *m*				les fruits tropicaux
mûr *m*	mou *m*	séchée *f*	cru *m*	de saison	complet *m*	tropical fruit
mûre *f*	molle *f*	desiccated	crue *f*	seasonal	complète *f*	
ripe	soft		raw		whole	le jacque
						jackfruit

les céréales et les légumineuses • grains and legumes

les céréales • grains

le blé
wheat

l'avoine
oats

l'orge
barley

le millet
millet

le maïs
corn

le quinoa
quinoa

vocabulaire • vocabulary

la graine seed	frais *m* fraîche *f* fresh	facile à cuisiner quick cooking
l'enveloppe husk	parfumé *m* parfumée *f* fragranced	à grains longs long-grain
le grain kernel		
la céréale cereal	complet *m* complète *f* whole-grain	à grains ronds short-grain
sec *m* sèche *f* dry	laisser tremper soak (v)	

le riz • rice

les céréales transformées
processed grains

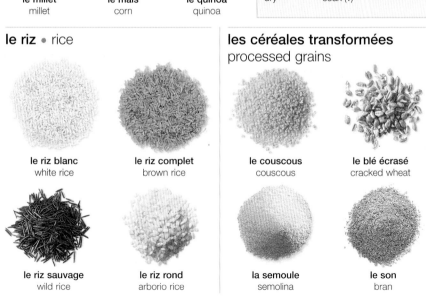

le riz blanc
white rice

le riz complet
brown rice

le couscous
couscous

le blé écrasé
cracked wheat

le riz sauvage
wild rice

le riz rond
arborio rice

la semoule
semolina

le son
bran

les légumineuses • legumes

**les haricots
de Lima**
butter beans

**les haricots
blancs**
haricot beans

**les haricots
rouges**
red kidney beans

**les haricots
azuki**
adzuki beans

les fèves
fava beans

**les graines
de soja**
soybeans

**les haricots
à œil noir**
black-eyed peas

**les haricots
pinto**
pinto beans

**les haricots
mungo**
mung beans

les flageolets
flageolet beans

les lentilles
brown lentils

les lentilles corail
red lentils

les petits pois
green peas

les pois chiches
chickpeas

les pois cassés
split peas

les graines • seeds

**la graine
de courge**
pumpkin seed

**le grain
de moutarde**
mustard seed

**la graine
de carvi**
caraway seed

**la graine
de sésame**
sesame seed

la graine de tournesol
sunflower seed

les herbes et les épices • herbs and spices
les épices • spices

la vanille
vanilla

la noix de muscade
nutmeg

le macis
mace

le curcuma
turmeric

le cumin
cumin

le bouquet garni
bouquet garni

le poivre de la Jamaïque
allspice

le grain de poivre
peppercorn

le fenugrec
fenugreek

le piment
chili powder

entier *m*
entière *f*
whole

écrasé *m*
écrasée *f*
crushed

le safran
saffron

la cardamome
cardamom

la poudre de curry
curry powder

moulu
ground

le paprika
paprika

en flocons
flakes

l'ail
garlic

les herbes • herbs

les bâtons
sticks

la cannelle
cinnamon

le fenouil
fennel

les graines
de fenouil
fennel seeds

la feuille de laurier
bay leaf

le persil
parsley

la citronnelle
lemongrass

la ciboulette
chives

la menthe
mint

le thym
thyme

la sauge
sage

le clou de girofle
cloves

l'estragon
tarragon

la marjolaine
marjoram

le basilic
basil

l'anis étoilé
star anise

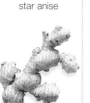

le gingembre
ginger

l'origan
oregano

la coriandre
cilantro

l'aneth
dill

le romarin
rosemary

les aliments en bouteilles et bocaux
bottled foods

l'huile de noix
walnut oil

l'huile de pépins de raisin
grapeseed oil

le bouchon
cork

l'huile de tournesol
sunflower oil

l'huile d'amande
almond oil

l'huile de sésame
sesame seed oil

l'huile de noisette
hazelnut oil

l'huile d'olive
olive oil

les herbes
herbs

l'huile parfumée
flavored oil

les huiles
oils

les produits à tartiner • sweet spreads

le pot
jar

le gâteau de miel
honeycomb

le miel solide
raw honey

la pâte à tartiner au citron
lemon curd

la confiture de framboises
raspberry jam

la confiture d'oranges
marmalade

le miel liquide
clear honey

le sirop d'érable
maple syrup

les sauces et les condiments
sauces and condiments

la bouteille
bottle

le vinaigre
de cidre
cider vinegar

le vinaigre
balsamique
balsamic vinegar

la moutarde
anglaise
English mustard

la mayonnaise
mayonnaise

le ketchup
ketchup

la moutarde
française
Dijon mustard

le chutney
chutney

le vinaigre de malt
malt vinegar

le vinaigre de vin
wine vinegar

la sauce
sauce

la moutarde
en grains
whole-grain
mustard

le vinaigre
vinegar

---

le bocal scellé
canning jar

le beurre de
cacahouètes
peanut butter

la pâte à tartiner
au chocolat
chocolate spread

les fruits
en bocaux
preserved fruit

vocabulaire • vocabulary

l'huile de maïs corn oil	l'huile de colza canola oil
l'huile d'arachide peanut oil	l'huile pressée à froid cold-pressed oil
l'huile végétale vegetable oil	la sauce soja soy sauce

les produits laitiers • dairy products

le fromage • cheese

la croûte
rind

le fromage à pâte
pressée non cuite
semi-hard cheese

le fromage râpé
grated cheese

le fromage à pâte pressée cuite
hard cheese

le fromage
blanc
cottage
cheese

le fromage à pâte
semi-molle
semi-soft cheese

le fromage
frais à tartiner
cream cheese

le bleu
blue cheese

le fromage à pâte molle
soft cheese

le fromage frais | fresh cheese

le lait • milk

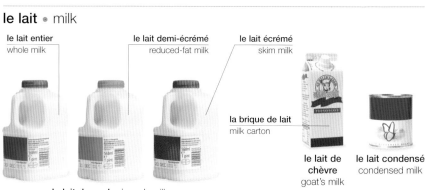

le lait entier
whole milk

le lait demi-écrémé
reduced-fat milk

le lait écrémé
skim milk

la brique de lait
milk carton

le lait de
chèvre
goat's milk

le lait condensé
condensed milk

le lait de vache | cow's milk

le beurre
butter

la margarine
margarine

la crème
cream

la crème liquide
half-and-half

**la crème
épaisse**
heavy cream

**la crème
fouettée**
whipped cream

la crème fraîche
sour cream

le yaourt
yogurt

la glace
ice cream

les œufs • eggs

le jaune d'œuf
egg yolk

le blanc d'œuf
egg white

la coquille
shell

**le
coquetier**
eggcup

l'œuf à la coque | soft-boiled egg

l'œuf de poule
hen's egg

l'œuf de cane
duck egg

l'œuf d'oie
goose egg

l'œuf de caille
quail egg

vocabulaire • vocabulary

pasteurisé pasteurized	**le milk-shake** milk shake	**salé** *m* **salée** *f* salted	**le lait d'avoine** oat milk	**le lactose** lactose	**le lait le babeurre** buttermilk
non pasteurisé unpasteurized	**le yaourt glacé** frozen yogurt	**non salé** *m* **non salée** *f* unsalted	**le lait d'amande** almond milk	**sans matières grasses** fat-free	**le lait en poudre** powdered milk

les pains et la farine • breads and flours

le pain
loaf

la baguette
baguette

la ciabatta
ciabatta

le pain
de seigle
rye bread

le croissant
croissant

la boulangerie | bakery

faire du pain • making bread

la farine blanche
white flour

**la farine
semi-complète**
brown flour

la farine complète
whole-wheat flour

la levure
yeast

tamiser | sift (v)

la pâte
dough

mélanger | mix (v)

pétrir | knead (v)

faire cuire au four | bake (v)

la croûte
crust

le pain blanc
white bread

le pain
loaf

le pain complet
brown bread

le pain de son
whole-wheat bread

la tranche
slice

le pain aux céréales
multigrain bread

le pain de maïs
corn bread

**le pain au bicarbonate
de soude**
soda bread

le pain au levain
sourdough bread

le pain plat
flat bread

le bagel
bagel

le petit pain rond
bun

le petit pain
roll

le pain aux fruits secs
fruit bread

le pain aux graines
seeded bread

le naan
naan bread

le pita
pita bread

la biscotte
crispbread

---

vocabulaire • vocabulary

la farine forte bread flour	**monter** rise (v)	**lever** prove (v)	**la chapelure** breadcrumbs	**la trancheuse** slicer
la farine avec la levure self-rising flour	**la farine sans levure** all-purpose flour	**sans gluten** gluten-free	**la flûte** flute	**le boulanger** *m* **la boulangère** *f* baker

les gâteaux et les desserts • cakes and desserts

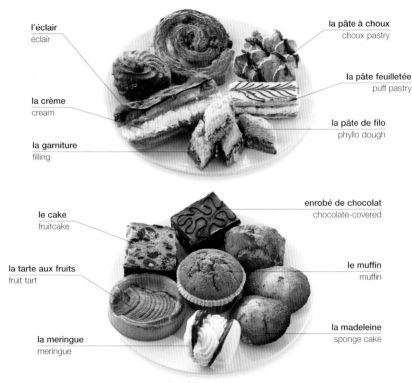

l'éclair
éclair

la pâte à choux
choux pastry

la pâte feuilletée
puff pastry

la crème
cream

la pâte de filo
phyllo dough

la garniture
filling

enrobé de chocolat
chocolate-covered

le cake
fruitcake

la tarte aux fruits
fruit tart

le muffin
muffin

la madeleine
sponge cake

la meringue
meringue

la pâtisseries | cakes

---

vocabulaire • vocabulary

la crème pâtissière crème pâtissière	**le petit gâteau** bun	**la pâte** pastry	**le riz au lait** rice pudding	**Est-ce que je peux avoir une tranche s'il vous plaît?** May I have a slice, please?
le gâteau au chocolat chocolate cake	**la crème anglaise** custard	**la tranche** slice	**la fête** celebration	

---

français • english

la pépite de
chocolat
chocolate chip

les boudoirs
ladyfinger

le florentin
Florentine

le diplomate
trifle

les biscuits | cookies

la mousse
mousse

le sorbet
sherbet

la tarte à la crème
cream pie

la crème caramel
crème caramel

les gâteaux de fête • celebration cakes

l'étage supérieur
top tier

le ruban
ribbon

l'étage
inférieur
bottom tier

le glaçage
frosting

la pâte
d'amandes
marzipan

la
décoration
decoration

les bougies
d'anniversaire
birthday candles

souffler
blow out (v)

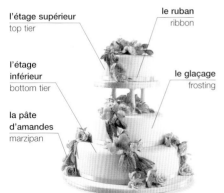

le gâteau de mariage | wedding cake

le gâteau d'anniversaire | birthday cake

la charcuterie • delicatessen

le saucisson piquant
spicy sausage

la quiche
quiche

le vinaigre
vinegar

l'huile
oil

la viande non cuite
uncooked meat

le comptoir
counter

le salami
salami

le pepperoni
pepperoni

le pâté
pâté

la mozzarella
mozzarella

le brie
Brie

le fromage de chèvre
goat cheese

le cheddar
cheddar

le parmesan
Parmesan

le camembert
Camembert

la croûte
rind

l'édam
Edam

le manchego
Manchego

les pâtés en croûte
meat pies

l'olive noire
black olive

le piment
chili pepper

la sauce
sauce

le petit pain
bread roll

la viande cuite
cooked meat

l'olive verte
green olive

le comptoir sandwichs
sandwich counter

le jambon
ham

le poisson fumé
smoked fish

les câpres
capers

vocabulaire • vocabulary

à l'huile in oil	salé m / salée f salted
en saumure in brine	fumé m / fumée f smoked
mariné m / marinée f marinated	séché m / séchée f cured

Prenez un numéro, s'il vous plaît.
Take a number, please.

Est-ce que je peut goûter un peu de ça, s'il vous plaît?
Can I try some of that, please?

Je voudrais six tranches, s'il vous plaît.
May I have six slices of that, please?

le prosciutto
prosciutto

le chorizo
chorizo

l'olive fourrée
stuffed olive

les boissons • drinks

l'eau • water

l'eau en bouteille
bottled water

gazeuse
sparkling

plate
still

l'eau minérale
mineral water

l'eau du robinet
tap water

le tonic
tonic water

l'eau pétillante
soda water

les boissons chaudes
hot drinks

le sachet de thé
teabag

les feuilles de thé
loose-leaf tea

le thé
tea

les grains
beans

le café moulu
ground coffee

le café
coffee

le chocolat chaud
hot chocolate

la boisson maltée
malted milk

les boissons non alcoolisées • soft drinks

la paille
straw

le jus de tomate
tomato juice

le jus de fruits
fruit juice

la limonade
lemonade

l'orangeade
orangeade

le coca
cola

les boissons alcoolisées • alcoholic drinks

le gin
gin

la boîte
can

la bière
beer

le cidre
hard cider

l'amer
amber ale

la bière brune
stout

la vodka
vodka

le whisky
whiskey

le rhum
rum

le brandy
brandy

le porto
port

sec
dry

le sherry
sherry

le saké
sake

rosé
rosé

blanc
white

rouge
red

le vin
wine

la liqueur
liqueur

la téquila
tequila

le champagne
champagne

sortir manger
eating out

le café • café

le store
awning

le menu
menu

la terrasse de café | sidewalk café

le parasol
umbrella

la terrasse
patio café

le percolateur
coffee machine

la table
table

le snack bar | snack bar

le café • coffee

le crème
coffee with milk

le noir
black coffee

le chocolat
en poudre
cocoa powder

la mousse
froth

le café filtre
filter coffee

l'expresso
espresso

le cappuccino
cappuccino

le café glacé
iced coffee

le thé • tea

la tisane
herbal tea

la camomille
chamomile tea

le thé vert
green tea

le thé au lait
tea with milk

le thé noir
black tea

le thé au citron
tea with lemon

le thé à la menthe
mint tea

le thé glacé
iced tea

les jus et milk-shakes • juices and milkshakes

le milk-shake au chocolat
chocolate milkshake

**le milk-shake
à la fraise**
strawberry
milkshake

**le milk-shake
au café**
coffee milkshake

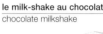

**le jus
d'orange**
orange juice

**le jus de
pomme**
apple juice

**le jus
d'ananas**
pineapple juice

**le jus de
tomate**
tomato juice

la nourriture • food

le pain complet
whole-wheat bread

la boule
scoop

le sandwich grillé
toasted sandwich

la salade
salad

la glace
ice cream

la pâtisserie
pastry

le bar • bar

le percolateur
coffee machine

la bière à la
pression
beer tap

le barman *m*
la barmaid *f*
bartender

la caisse
cash
register

le comptoir
bar counter

le dessous de verre
coaster

l'ouvre-bouteille
bottle opener

le levier
lever

les pinces
tongs

l'agitateur
stirrer

le verre
gradué
measure

le tire-bouchon
corkscrew

le shaker à cocktails | cocktail shaker

vocabulaire
vocabulary

le doseur
dispenser

le seau à glace
ice bucket

le cendrier
ashtray

le tabouret de bar
bar stool

le pichet
pitcher

le glaçon
ice cube

le gin tonic
gin and tonic

le scotch à l'eau
scotch and water

le rhum coca
rum and cola

la vodka à l'orange
screwdriver

le martini
martini

le cocktail
cocktail

le vin
wine

la bière | beer

simple
single

double
double

citron et glaçons
ice and lemon

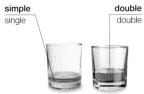

le shot
shot

la mesure
measure

sans glaçons
without ice

avec des glaçons
with ice

les amuse-gueule • bar snacks

**les noix
de cajou**
cashews

**les
cacahouètes**
peanuts

les amandes
almonds

les chips | potato chips

les noix | nuts

les olives | olives

le restaurant • restaurant

il coperto
table setting

le commis *m*
la commise *f*
sous chef

le chef *m*
la cheffe *f*
chef

le verre
glass

le plateau
tray

la cuisine
kitchen

le serveur *m* / **la serveuse** *f*
server

vocabulaire • vocabulary

le menu du soir dinner menu	**les spécialités** specials	**le prix** price	**le pourboire** tip	**le sel** salt	**le bar** bar
la carte des vins wine list	**à la carte** à la carte	**l'addition** check	**service compris** service charge not included	**le poivre** pepper	**le client** *m* **la cliente** *f* customer
le menu du déjeuner lunch menu	**le plateau de desserts** dessert cart	**le reçu** receipt	**service non compris** service charge included	**le buffet** buffet	

la carte
menu

le menu enfant
child's meal

commander
order (v)

payer
pay (v)

les plats • courses

l'apéritif
apéritif

l'entrée
appetizer

la soupe
soup

le plat principal
entrée

l'accompagnement
side dish

le dessert | dessert

le café | coffee

---

vocabulaire • vocabulary

**Une table pour deux,
s'il vous plaît.**
A table for two, please.

**La carte / la carte des vins,
s'il vous plaît.**
Can I see the menu / wine list,
please?

Avez-vous un menu à prix fixe?
Is there a fixed-price menu?

**Avez vous des plats
végétariens?**
Do you have any vegetarian
dishes?

**L'addition / un reçu, s'il
vous plaît.**
Could I have the check / a receipt,
please?

**Pouvons-nous payer chacun
notre part?**
Can we pay separately?

**Où sont les toilettes,
s'il vous plaît?**
Where is the restroom, please?

---

la restauration rapide • fast food

la paille
straw

le hamburger
burger

la boisson
non-alcoolisée
soft drink

les frites
French fries

la serviette
en papier
paper napkin

le plateau
tray

le hamburger avec des frites
burger meal

vocabulaire
vocabulary

la pizzeria
pizzeria

le restaurant rapide
burger bar

la carte
menu

manger sur place
eat in

à emporter
to go

réchauffer
reheat (v)

le ketchup
ketchup

**À emporter, s'il
vous plaît.**
Can I have that to go,
please?

**Est-ce que vous livrez
à domicile?**
Do you deliver?

la boisson en boîte
canned drink

le tarif
price list

la livraison à domicile
home delivery

le food truck
street vendor

le petit pain
bun

la moutarde
mustard

la saucisse
sausage

le hamburger
hamburger

le hamburger au poulet
chicken sandwich

le hamburger végétarien
veggie burger

le hot-dog
hot dog

le sandwich
sandwich

le club sandwich
club sandwich

la garniture
filling

la tartine
open-faced sandwich

le wrap
wrap

la sauce
sauce

salé *m*
salée *f*
savory

sucré *m*
sucrée *f*
sweet

la garniture
topping

les brochettes
kebab

les beignets de poulet
chicken nuggets

les crêpes | crepes

le fish and chips
fish and chips

les côtes
ribs

le poulet frit
fried chicken

la pizza
pizza

le petit déjeuner • breakfast

le lait	les céréales	la confiture	les fruit secs	le jambon	le fromage	les biscottes
milk	cereal	jam	dried fruit	ham	cheese	crispbread

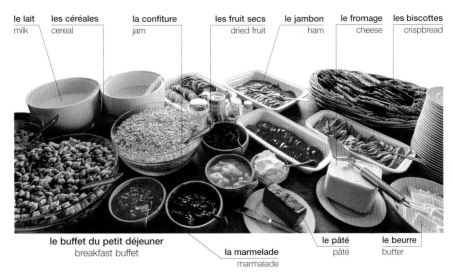

le buffet du petit déjeuner
breakfast buffet

la marmelade
marmalade

le pâté
pâté

le beurre
butter

le jus de fruit
fruit juice

le café
coffee

le chocolat chaud
hot chocolate

le croissant
croissant

le thé
tea

la table du petit déjeuner | breakfast table

les boissons | drinks

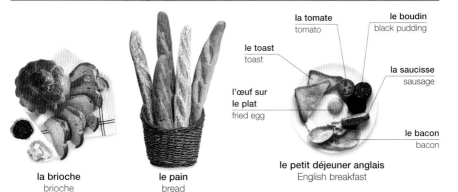

la tomate
tomato

le boudin
black pudding

le toast
toast

la saucisse
sausage

l'œuf sur
le plat
fried egg

le bacon
bacon

le petit déjeuner anglais
English breakfast

la brioche
brioche

le pain
bread

le jaune d'œuf
egg yolk

le blanc d'œuf
egg white

le hareng fumé
kippers

le pain perdu
French toast

l'œuf à la coque
soft-boiled egg

les œufs brouillés
scrambled eggs

la crème
whipped cream

le yaourt aux fruits
fruit yogurt

les crêpes
crepes

les gaufres
waffles

le porridge
oatmeal

les fruits
fresh fruit

le repas • dinner

le potage
soup

le bouillon
broth

le ragoût
stew

le curry
curry

le rôti
roast

la tourte
pie

le soufflé
soufflé

la brochette
kebab

les nouilles
noodles

les baguettes
chopsticks

**les boulettes
de viande**
meatballs

l'omelette
omelet

le sauté
stir-fry

les pâtes
pasta

le riz
rice

la salade composée
tossed salad

la salade verte
green salad

la vinaigrette
dressing

la préparation • techniques

farci *m* / **farcie** *f*
stuffed

en sauce
in sauce

grillé *m* / **grillée** *f*
grilled

mariné *m* / **marinée** *f*
marinated

poché *m* / **pochée** *f*
poached

écrasé *m* / **écrasée** *f*
mashed

cuit au four *m*
cuite au four *f*
baked

sauté *m* / **sautée** *f*
pan-fried

frit à la poêle *m*
frite à la poêle *f*
fried

au vinaigre
pickled

fumé *m* / **fumée** *f*
smoked

frit *m* / **frite** *f*
deep-fried

au sirop
in syrup

assaisonné *m*
assaisonnée *f*
dressed

cuit à la vapeur *m*
cuite à la vapeur *f*
steamed

séché *m* / **séchée** *f*
cured

l'éducation
study

l'école • school

le tableau blanc
whiteboard

le professeur *m*
la professeure *f*
teacher

le cartable
school
backpack

le pupitre
desk

la salle de classe | classroom

l'élève *m/f*
student

vocabulaire • vocabulary

l'histoire history	**les sciences** science	**la physique** physics
les langues languages	**l'art** art	**la chimie** chemistry
la littérature literature	**la musique** music	**la biologie** biology
la géographie geography	**les mathématiques** math	**l'éducation physique** physical education

les activités • activities

lire | read (v)

écrire | write (v)

orthographier
spell (v)

dessiner
draw (v)

la pointe
nib

le crayon de couleur
colored pencil

le taille-crayon
pencil sharpener

le vidéoprojecteur
digital projector

le stylo
pen

le crayon
pencil

le cahier
notebook

la gomme
eraser

le manuel
textbook

la trousse
pencil case

la règle
ruler

questionner
question (v)

répondre
answer (v)

discuter
discuss (v)

apprendre
learn (v)

vocabulaire • vocabulary

le professeur principal *m* **la professeure principale** *f* principal	**la question** question	**la note** grade
	la réponse answer	**la classe** year
la leçon lesson	**l'examen** test	**le dictionnaire** dictionary
les devoirs homework	**la rédaction** essay	**l'encyclopédie** encyclopedia
prendre des notes take notes (v)		

les mathématiques • math

les formes • shapes

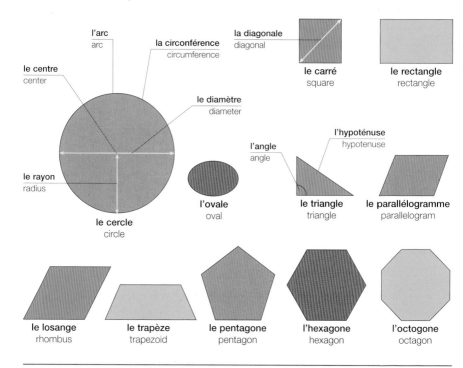

l'arc
arc

la circonférence
circumference

la diagonale
diagonal

le carré
square

le rectangle
rectangle

le centre
center

le diamètre
diameter

l'hypoténuse
hypotenuse

l'angle
angle

le rayon
radius

l'ovale
oval

le triangle
triangle

le parallélogramme
parallelogram

le cercle
circle

le losange
rhombus

le trapèze
trapezoid

le pentagone
pentagon

l'hexagone
hexagon

l'octogone
octagon

les solides • solids

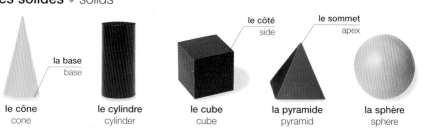

le côté
side

le sommet
apex

la base
base

le cône
cone

le cylindre
cylinder

le cube
cube

la pyramide
pyramid

la sphère
sphere

les lignes • lines

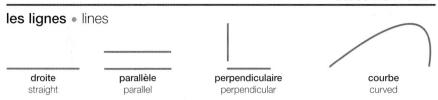

droite	parallèle	perpendiculaire	courbe
straight	parallel	perpendicular	curved

les mesures • measurements

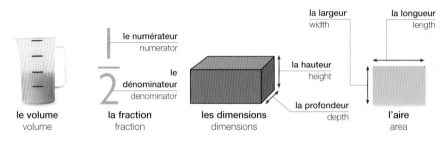

le volume
volume

la fraction
fraction

le numérateur
numerator

le dénominateur
denominator

les dimensions
dimensions

la largeur
width

la longueur
length

la hauteur
height

la profondeur
depth

l'aire
area

l'équipement • equipment

l'équerre	le rapporteur	la règle	le compas	la calculatrice
triangle	protractor	ruler	compass	calculator

vocabulaire • vocabulary

la géométrie	plus	fois	égale(nt)	additionner	multiplier	l'équation
geometry	plus	times	equals	add (v)	multiply (v)	equation
l'arithmétique	moins	divisé par	compter	soustraire	diviser	le pourcentage
arithmetic	minus	divided by	count (v)	subtract (v)	divide (v)	percentage

la science • science

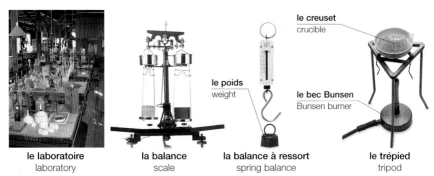

le laboratoire
laboratory

la balance
scale

la balance à ressort
spring balance

le poids
weight

le creuset
crucible

le bec Bunsen
Bunsen burner

le trépied
tripod

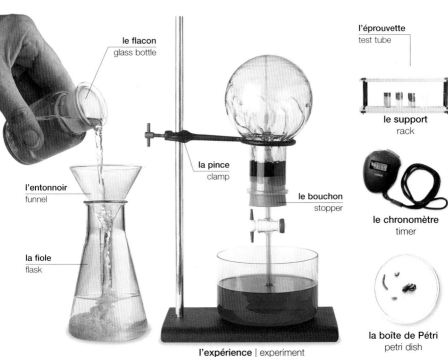

le flacon
glass bottle

l'entonnoir
funnel

la fiole
flask

la pince
clamp

le bouchon
stopper

l'éprouvette
test tube

le support
rack

le chronomètre
timer

la boîte de Pétri
petri dish

l'expérience | experiment

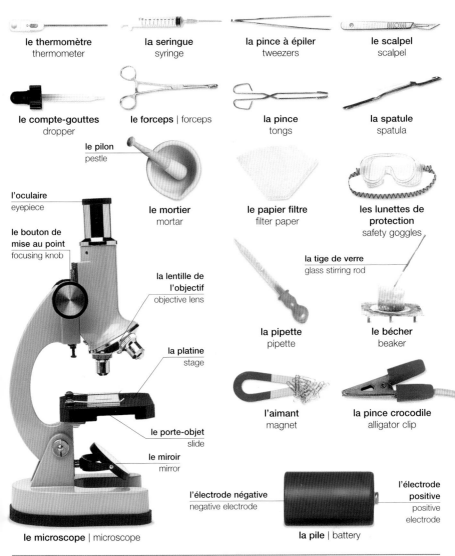

le thermomètre
thermometer

la seringue
syringe

la pince à épiler
tweezers

le scalpel
scalpel

le compte-gouttes
dropper

le forceps | forceps

la pince
tongs

la spatule
spatula

le pilon
pestle

l'oculaire
eyepiece

le bouton de
mise au point
focusing knob

le mortier
mortar

le papier filtre
filter paper

les lunettes de
protection
safety goggles

la lentille de
l'objectif
objective lens

la tige de verre
glass stirring rod

la pipette
pipette

le bécher
beaker

la platine
stage

le porte-objet
slide

le miroir
mirror

l'aimant
magnet

la pince crocodile
alligator clip

l'électrode négative
negative electrode

l'électrode
positive
positive
electrode

le microscope | microscope

la pile | battery

l'université • college

le terrain
de sport
playing field

le restaurant
universitaire
cafeteria

le service
de santé
health center

la résidence
universitaire
residence hall

le secrétariat
admissions
office

le campus | campus

le bibliothécaire *m*
la bibliothécaire *f*
librarian

le service de prêt
circulation desk

l'étagère
à livres
bookshelf

le périodique
periodical

la revue
journal

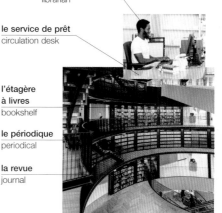

la bibliothèque | library

vocabulaire • vocabulary

la carte de bibliothèque library card	les renseignements help desk	le prêt loan
la salle de lecture reading room	emprunter borrow (v)	le livre book
les ouvrages recommandés reading list	réserver reserve (v)	le titre title
la date de retour due date	renouveler renew (v)	le couloir aisle

le professeur m
la professeure f
professor

l'étudiant m
l'étudiante f
undergraduate

le diplômé m
la diplômée f
graduate

la robe
gown

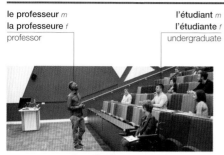

la salle de cours
lecture hall

la cérémonie de la remise des diplômes
graduation ceremony

les écoles • schools

le modèle m/f
model

l'école des beaux arts
art school

le Conservatoire
music school

l'école de danse
dance school

vocabulaire • vocabulary

la bourse scholarship	la recherche research	le mémoire dissertation	la médecine medicine	la philosophie philosophy
le diplôme diploma	le master master's	l'UFR department	la zoologie zoology	la littérature literature
la licence degree	le doctorat doctorate	le droit law	la physique physics	l'histoire de l'art art history
le doctorant m la doctorante f postgraduate	la thèse thesis	les études d'ingénieur engineering	les sciences politiques political science	les sciences économiques economics

le travail
work

le bureau • office (1)

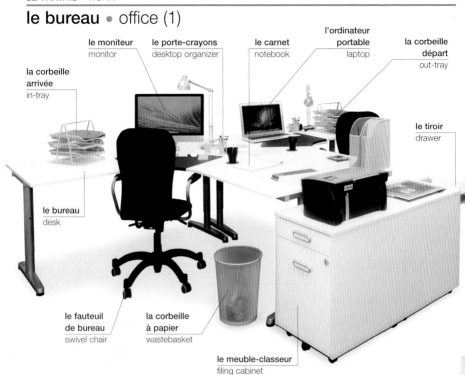

la corbeille
arrivée
in-tray

le moniteur
monitor

le porte-crayons
desktop organizer

le carnet
notebook

l'ordinateur
portable
laptop

la corbeille
départ
out-tray

le tiroir
drawer

le bureau
desk

le fauteuil
de bureau
swivel chair

la corbeille
à papier
wastebasket

le meuble-classeur
filing cabinet

l'équipement de bureau • office equipment

le bac à
papier
paper tray

l'imprimante | printer

le destructeur de documents
shredder

vocabulaire • vocabulary

imprimer
print (v)

agrandir
enlarge (v)

photocopier
copy (v)

réduire
reduce (v)

**J'ai besoin de faire des
photocopies.**
I need to make some copies.

les fournitures de bureau • office supplies

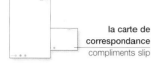

la carte de
correspondance
compliments slip

le papier à lettres
letterhead

l'enveloppe
envelope

le dossier-classeur
box file

la fiche intercalaire
divider

l'étiquette
tab

le porte-bloc
clipboard

le bloc-notes
notepad

le dossier suspendu
hanging file

le porte-dossiers
expanding file

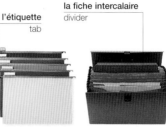

**le classeur
à levier**
binder

les agrafes
staples

le scotch
tape

le tampon encreur
ink pad

l'agenda
personal organizer

l'agrafeuse
stapler

**le dévidoir de
scotch**
tape dispenser

le perforateur
hole punch

le cachet
rubber stamp

l'élastique
rubber band

la pince à dessin
bulldog clip

le trombone
paper clip

la punaise
thumbtack

le panneau d'affichage | bulletin board

le bureau • office (2)

le tableau de
conférence
flip chart

le chevalet
easel

le responsable *m*
la responsable *f*
manager

la proposition
proposal

le compte
rendu
minutes

le rapport
report

le cadre *m*
la cadre *f*
executive

la réunion | meeting

vocabulaire • vocabulary

la salle de conférence
meeting room

assister à
attend (v)

l'ordre du jour
agenda

présider
chair (v)

La conférence est à quelle heure?
What time is the meeting?

Quelles sont vos heures de bureau?
What are your office hours?

le présentateur *m*
la présentatrice *f*
speaker

la présentation | presentation

les affaires • business

l'homme d'affaires *m*
businessman / businessperson

la femme d'affaires *f*
businesswoman / businessperson

le déjeuner d'affaires
business lunch

le voyage d'affaires
business trip

le rendez-vous
appointment

le directeur général *m*
la directrice générale *f*
CEO

l'agenda électronique | digital calendar

le client *m*
la cliente *f*
client

le contrat
business deal

---

vocabulaire • vocabulary

la société
company

le siège social
head office

la succursale
regional office

le personnel
staff

le salaire
salary

les effectifs
payroll

la comptabilité
accounting department

le service marketing
marketing department

le service des ventes
sales department

le service juridique
legal department

le service après-vente
customer service department

le service des ressources humaines
human resources department

---

l'ordinateur • computer

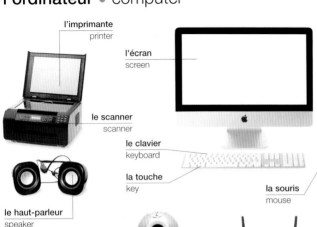

l'imprimante
printer

l'écran
screen

le scanner
scanner

le clavier
keyboard

la touche
key

la souris
mouse

l'ordinateur portable
laptop

le haut-parleur
speaker

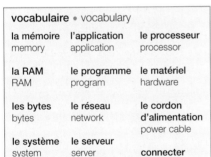

le casque sans fil
bluetooth headset

la webcam
webcam

le routeur
router

la clé USB
memory stick

le disque dur externe
external hard drive

vocabulaire • vocabulary

la mémoire memory	**l'application** application	**le processeur** processor
la RAM RAM	**le programme** program	**le matériel** hardware
les bytes bytes	**le réseau** network	**le cordon d'alimentation** power cable
le système system	**le serveur** server	**connecter** connect (v)
le logiciel software	**le port** port	

la batterie
battery pack

la tablette
tablet

le cordon de charge
charging cable

le smartphone
smartphone

le bureau • desktop

la barre
de menus
menu bar

la police
de caractères
font

la barre d'outils
toolbar

l'icône
icon

la fenêtre
window

le fichier
file

le dossier
folder

la corbeille
trash

---

l'internet • internet

le site web
website

le navigateur
browser

naviguer
browse (v)

l'e-mail • email

la boîte de
réception
inbox

l'adresse
e-mail
email address

---

vocabulaire • vocabulary

installer install (v)	**se connecter** log on (v)	**le mot de passe** password	**le stockage dans le cloud** cloud storage	**envoyer** send (v)	**sauvegarder** save (v)
en ligne online	**le fournisseur d'accès** service provider	**télécharger** download (v)	**la pièce jointe** attachment	**recevoir** receive (v)	**chercher** search (v)

---

les médias • media

le studio de télévision • television studio

le plateau
set

le présentateur *m*
la présentatrice *f*
host

l'éclairage
light

la caméra
camera

la grue de caméra
camera crane

le caméraman *m*
la caméraman *f*
camera operator

---

vocabulaire • vocabulary

la chaîne channel	le journal **télévisé** news	la presse press	le feuilleton soap opera	le dessin animé cartoon	en direct live
la **programmation** programming	le documentaire documentary	la série télévisée television series	le jeu télévisé game show	en différé prerecorded	émettre broadcast (v)

l'interviewer *m/f*
interviewer

le journaliste *m*
la journaliste *f*
reporter

le prompteur
teleprompter

le présentateur *m*
la présentatrice *f*
anchor

les acteurs
actors

la perche
sound boom

le clap
clapper board

le décor de cinéma
movie set

la radio • radio

l'ingénieur du son *m*
l'ingénieure du son *f*
sound technician

la console
de mixage
mixing desk

le
microphone
microphone

le studio d'enregistrement | recording studio

vocabulaire • vocabulary

la station de radio radio station	le volume volume
le DJ *m* / la DJ *f* DJ	régler tune (v)
l'émission broadcast	analogique analog
la longueur d'ondes wavelength	numérique digital
la fréquence frequency	

le droit • law

l'huissier de justice *m*
l'huissière de justice *f*
bailiff

l'avocat *m*
l'avocate *f*
lawyer

le jury
jury

le banc
des jurés
jury box

le témoin *m*
la témoin *f*
witness

le juge *m*
la juge *f*
judge

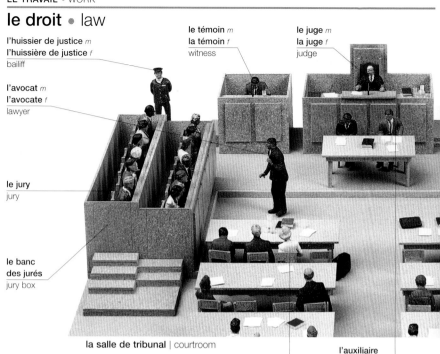

la salle de tribunal | courtroom

l'accusation
prosecution

l'auxiliaire
de justice *m/f*
court clerk

---

vocabulaire • vocabulary

le cabinet d'avocat lawyer's office	l'assignation summons	l'acte judiciaire writ	l'affaire court case
le conseil juridique legal advice	la déposition statement	la date du procès court date	l'accusation charge
le client *m* la cliente *f* client	le mandat warrant	le plaidoyer plea	l'accusé *m* l'accusée *f* accused

---

le sténographe *m*
la sténographe *f*
stenographer

le suspect *m*
la suspecte *f*
suspect

le criminel *m*
la criminelle *f*
criminal

la défense *f*
defense

l'accusé *m*
l'accusée *f*
defendant

le portrait-robot
composite sketch

le casier judiciaire
criminal record

le gardien de prison *m*
la gardienne de prison *f*
prison guard

la cellule
cell

la prison
prison

vocabulaire • vocabulary

la preuve evidence	**innocent** *m* **innocente** *f* innocent	**la caution** bail	**Je voudrais voir un avocat.** I want to see a lawyer.
le verdict verdict	**acquitté** *m* **acquittée** *f* acquitted	**l'appel** appeal	**Où est le palais de justice?** Where is the courthouse?
coupable guilty	**la condamnation** sentence	**la liberté conditionnelle** parole	**Est-ce que je peux verser la caution?** Can I post bail?

la ferme • farm (1)

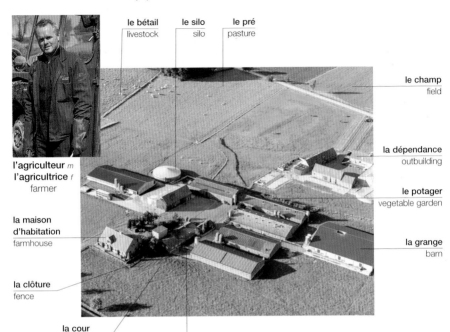

le bétail
livestock

le silo
silo

le pré
pasture

le champ
field

la dépendance
outbuilding

l'agriculteur *m*
l'agricultrice *f*
farmer

le potager
vegetable garden

la maison
d'habitation
farmhouse

la grange
barn

la clôture
fence

la cour
de ferme
farmyard

la barrière
gate

le tracteur | tractor

la moissonneuse-batteuse | combine

les exploitations agricoles • types of farms

la culture
crop

la ferme de culture
crop farm

la ferme laitière
dairy farm

le troupeau
flock

**la ferme d'élevage
de moutons**
sheep farm

la ferme d'aviculture
poultry farm

**la ferme
d'élevage porcin**
pig farm

**le centre de
pisciculture**
fish farm

l'exploitation fruitière
fruit farm

la vigne
vine

la viticulture
vineyard

les activités • actions

le sillon
furrow

labourer
plow (v)

semer
sow (v)

traire
milk (v)

donner à manger
feed (v)

arroser | water (v)

récolter | harvest (v)

vocabulaire • vocabulary		
l'herbicide herbicide	**le troupeau** herd	**l'auge** trough
le pesticide pesticide	**la haie** hedge	**planter** plant (v)

la ferme • farm (2)
les cultures • crops

le blé
wheat

le maïs
corn

l'orge
barley

le colza
rapeseed

le tournesol
sunflower

la balle
bale

le foin
hay

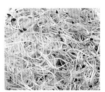

la luzerne
alfalfa

le tabac
tobacco

le riz
rice

le thé
tea

le café
coffee

le lin
flax

la canne à sucre
sugarcane

le coton
cotton

l'épouvantail
scarecrow

le bétail • livestock

le porcelet
piglet

le cochon
pig

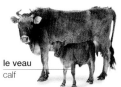

le veau
calf

la vache
cow

le taureau
bull

le mouton
sheep

l'agneau
lamb

le chevreau
kid

la chèvre
goat

le poulain
foal

le cheval
horse

l'âne
donkey

le poussin
chick

la poule
chicken

le coq
rooster

le dindon
turkey

le caneton
duckling

le canard
duck

l'écurie
stable

l'enclos
pen

le poulailler
chicken coop

la porcherie
pigsty

la construction
construction

le mur
wall

la poutre
beam

l'échafaudage
scaffolding

le chevron
rafter

la palette
pallet

le chantier
construction site

la fenêtre
window

l'échelle
ladder

la poutre
métallique
girder

le casque
de sécurité
hard hat

construire
build (v)

la ceinture
à outils
toolbelt

l'ouvrier du bâtiment *m*
l'ouvrière du bâtiment *f*
construction worker

le ciment
cement

la bétonnière
cement mixer

les matériaux • materials

la brique
brick

le bois
lumber

la tuile
roof tile

le parpaing
cinder block

les outils • tools

le mortier
mortar

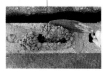
la truelle
trowel

le niveau à bulle
level

le manche
handle

la masse
sledgehammer

la pioche
pickax

la pelle
shovel

les machines
machinery

le rouleau compresseur
road roller

le tombereau
dump truck

le support
support

le
crochet
hook

la grue | crane

les travaux • roadwork

le macadam
asphalt

le cône
cone

**le marteau-
piqueur**
jackhammer

le
revêtement
resurfacing

**la pelle
mécanique**
excavator

les professions • occupations (1)

le menuisier *m*
la menuisière *f*
carpenter

l'électricien *m*
l'électrienne *f*
electrician

le plombier *m*
la plombière *f*
plumber

l'ouvrier du bâtiment *m*
l'ouvrière du bâtiment *f*
construction worker

le mécanicien *m*
la mécanicienne *f*
mechanic

le boucher *m*
la bouchère *f*
butcher

le pêcheur *m*
la pêcheuse *f*
fisherman / fisherwoman

le fleuriste *m*
la fleuriste *f*
florist

le bijoutier *m*
la bijoutière *f*
jeweler

le jardinier *m*
la jardinière *f*
gardener

le coiffeur *m*
la coiffeuse *f*
hairdresser

le barbier *m*
la barbière *f*
barber

l'employé de magasin *m*
l'employée de magasin *f*
salesperson

le moniteur de conduite *m*
la monitrice de conduite *f*
driving instructor

l'aspirateur
vacuum
cleaner

l'homme de ménage *m*
la femme de ménage *f*
cleaner

le géomètre *m*
la géomètre *f*
surveyor

le pharmacien m
la pharmacienne f
pharmacist

l'opticien m
l'opticienne f
optometrist

le masque
mask

le dentiste m
la dentiste f
dentist

le médecin m
la médecin f
doctor

l'infirmier m
l'infirmière f
nurse

le vétérinaire m
la vétérinaire f
veterinarian

le kinésithérapeute m
la kinésithérapeute f
physical therapist

le pompier m
la pompière f
firefighter

l'uniforme
uniform

le soldat m
la soldate f
soldier

le policier m
la policière f
police officer

le badge
badge

le vigile m
la femme vigile f
security guard

le marin m
la femme marin f
sailor

vocabulaire • vocabulary

le directeur du marketing m
la directrice du marketing f
marketing executive

le chargé des relations publiques m
la chargée des relations publiques f
public relations (PR) executive

l'interprète m/f
interpreter

le développeur d'application m
la développeuse d'application f
app developer

l'entrepreneur m
l'entrepreneuse f
entrepreneur

l'assistant de direction m
l'assistante de direction f
personal assistant (PA)

le concepteur web m
la conceptrice web f
web designer

les professions • occupations (2)

l'avocat *m*
l'avocate *f*
lawyer

le comptable *m*
la comptable *f*
accountant

la maquette
model

l'architecte *m/f*
architect

l'analyste de données *m/f*
data analyst

le scientifique *m*
la scientifique *f*
scientist

le professeur *m*
la professeure *f*
teacher

l'agent immobilier *m*
l'agente immobilière *f*
real estate agent

le réceptionniste *m*
la réceptionniste *f*
receptionist

le sac
postal
mailbag

le postier *m*
la postière *f*
mail carrier

le conducteur de bus *m*
la conductrice de bus *f*
bus driver

le camionneur *m*
la camionneuse *f*
truck driver

le chauffeur de taxi *m*
la chauffeuse de taxi *f*
taxi driver

le pilote *m*
la pilote *f*
pilot

le steward *m*
l'hôtesse de l'air *f*
flight attendant

le voyagiste *m*
la voyagiste *f*
travel agent

la toque
chef's hat

le chef *m*
la cheffe *f*
chef

le tutu
tutu

le musicien m
la musicienne f
musician

le danseur m
la danseuse f
dancer

l'acteur m
l'actrice f
actor

le chanteur m
la chanteuse f
singer

le serveur m
la serveuse f
server

le barman m
la barmaid f
bartender

le coach personnel m
la coach personnelle f
personal trainer

le sculpteur m
la sculptrice f
sculptor

le peintre m
la peintre f
painter

le photographe m
la photographe f
photographer

le présentateur m
la présentatrice f
anchor

les notes
notes

le journaliste m
la journaliste f
journalist

le rédacteur m
la rédactrice f
editor

le designer m
la designer f
designer

le couturier m
la couturière f
dressmaker

le tailleur m
la tailleuse f
tailor

le transport
transportation

les routes • roads

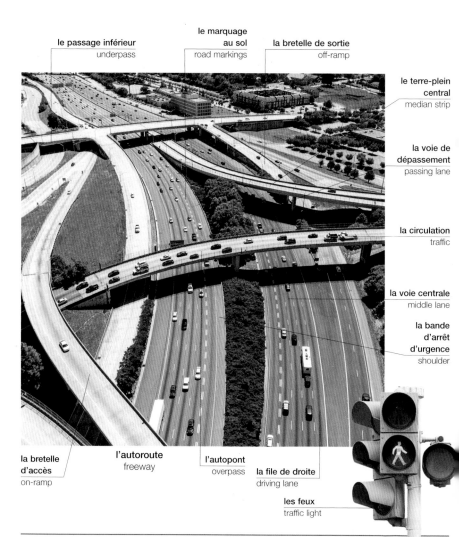

le passage inférieur
underpass

le marquage
au sol
road markings

la bretelle de sortie
off-ramp

le terre-plein
central
median strip

la voie de
dépassement
passing lane

la circulation
traffic

la voie centrale
middle lane

la bande
d'arrêt
d'urgence
shoulder

la bretelle
d'accès
on-ramp

l'autoroute
freeway

l'autopont
overpass

la file de droite
driving lane

les feux
traffic light

le passage clouté
crosswalk

le carrefour
interchange

**le téléphone
de secours**
emergency phone

le camion
truck

le parking réservé aux
**personnes
handicapées**
disabled parking

l'embouteillage
traffic jam

le parc-mètre
parking meter

**l'agent de
circulation** *m/f*
traffic police officer

vocabulaire · vocabulary

le rond-point roundabout	**le poste de péage** tollbooth	**remorquer** tow away (v)
la déviation detour	**doubler** pass (v)	**la rue à sens unique** one-way street
les travaux roadwork	**conduire** drive (v)	**la route à quatre voies** divided highway
la glissière de sécurité guardrail	**faire marche arrière** reverse (v)	**C'est la route pour… ?** Is this the road to… ?
garer park (v)		**Où peut-on se garer?** Where can I park?

les panneaux routiers · road signs

sens interdit
do not enter

**la limitation
de vitesse**
speed limit

danger
hazard

arrêt interdit
no stopping

**interdit de
tourner à droite**
no right turn

le bus • bus

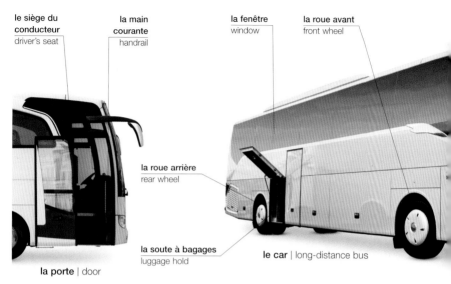

le siège du conducteur
driver's seat

la main courante
handrail

la fenêtre
window

la roue avant
front wheel

la roue arrière
rear wheel

la soute à bagages
luggage hold

le car | long-distance bus

la porte | door

les types de bus • types of buses

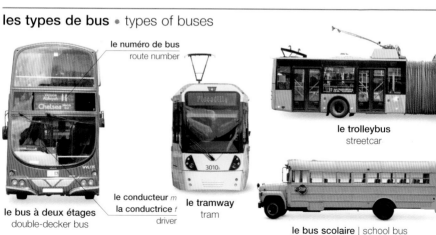

le numéro de bus
route number

le trolleybus
streetcar

le conducteur *m*
la conductrice *f*
driver

le tramway
tram

le bus à deux étages
double-decker bus

le bus scolaire | school bus

la porte automatique
automatic door

le bouton d'arrêt
stop button

le ticket
bus ticket

la sonnette
bell

la gare routière
bus station

l'arrêt de bus
bus stop

vocabulaire • vocabulary

le prix du ticket
fare

l'horaire
schedule

l'accès aux
handicapés
wheelchair access

l'abribus
bus shelter

Vous arrêtez à… ?
Do you stop at… ?

C'est quel bus pour
aller à… ?
Which bus goes to… ?

le minibus
minibus

la navette | shuttle bus

le bus de touristes | tour bus

la voiture • car (1)

l'extérieur • exterior

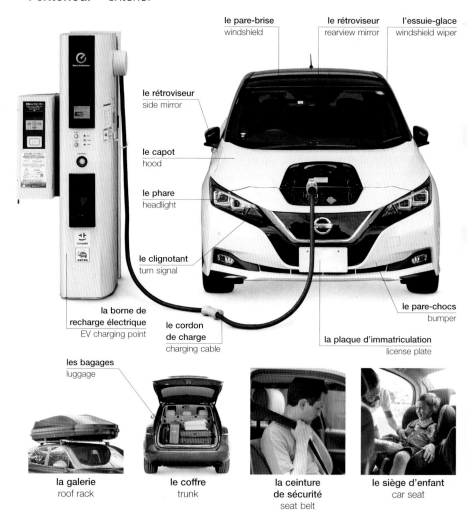

le pare-brise
windshield

le rétroviseur
rearview mirror

l'essuie-glace
windshield wiper

le rétroviseur
side mirror

le capot
hood

le phare
headlight

le clignotant
turn signal

la borne de
recharge électrique
EV charging point

le cordon
de charge
charging cable

le pare-chocs
bumper

la plaque d'immatriculation
license plate

les bagages
luggage

la galerie
roof rack

le coffre
trunk

la ceinture
de sécurité
seat belt

le siège d'enfant
car seat

les modèles · types

la voiture électrique
electric car

la porte
door
la voiture à hayon
hatchback

la berline
sedan

la roue
wheel
le break
station wagon

la décapotable
convertible

la voiture de sport
sports car

le monospace
minivan

le quatre-quatre
four-wheel drive

la voiture de collection
vintage

le pneu
tire
la limousine
limousine

la station-service · gas station

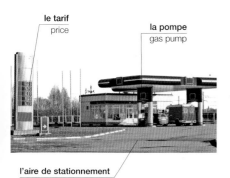
le tarif
price
la pompe
gas pump
l'aire de stationnement
entryway

vocabulaire · vocabulary

l'huile oil	**au plomb** leaded	**le lave-auto** car wash
l'essence gasoline	**le diesel** diesel	**l'antigel** antifreeze
sans plomb unleaded	**le garage** garage	**le lave-glace** windshield washer fluid

Le plein, s'il vous plaît.
Fill it up, please.

la voiture • car (2)

l'intérieur • interior

le siège arrière	l'accoudoir	le repose-tête	le verrouillage	la poignée
backseat	armrest	headrest	door lock	handle

vocabulaire • vocabulary

à deux portes	à quatre portes	automatique	le frein	l'accélérateur
two-door	four-door	automatic	brake	accelerator

à trois portes	manuel	l'allumage	l'embrayage	la climatisation
hatchback	manual	ignition	clutch	air-conditioning

Pouvez-vous m'indiquer la route pour… ?
Can you tell me the way to… ?

Où est le parking?
Where is the parking lot?

On peut se garer ici?
Can I park here?

les commandes • controls

le volant
steering wheel

le klaxon
horn

le tableau de bord
dashboard

le GPS
GPS

les feux
de détresse
hazard lights

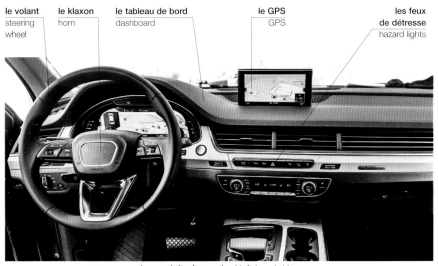

la conduite à gauche | left-hand drive

l'autoradio
car stereo

le compte-tours
tachometer

le compteur
de vitesse
speedometer

la jauge d'essence
fuel gauge

la jauge de
température
temperature gauge

l'interrupteur feux
light switch

le compteur
kilométrique
odometer

les boutons de réglage
du chauffage
heater controls

l'airbag
air bag

le levier de vitesses
gearshift

la conduite à droite | right-hand drive

la voiture • car (3)

la mécanique • mechanics

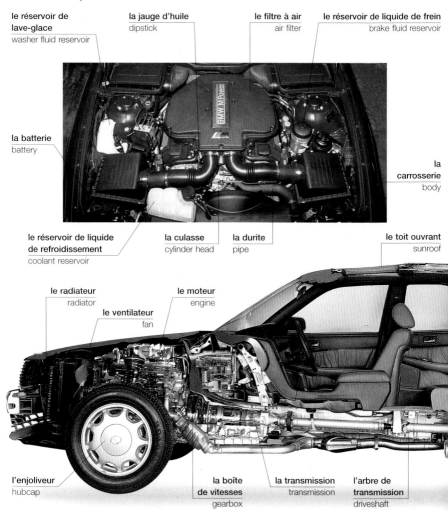

le réservoir de
lave-glace
washer fluid reservoir

la jauge d'huile
dipstick

le filtre à air
air filter

le réservoir de liquide de frein
brake fluid reservoir

la batterie
battery

la
carrosserie
body

le réservoir de liquide
de refroidissement
coolant reservoir

la culasse
cylinder head

la durite
pipe

le toit ouvrant
sunroof

le radiateur
radiator

le moteur
engine

le ventilateur
fan

l'enjoliveur
hubcap

la boîte
de vitesses
gearbox

la transmission
transmission

l'arbre de
transmission
driveshaft

la crevaison • flat tire

la roue de secours
spare tire

la manivelle
tire iron

les écrous de roue
lug nuts

le cric
jack

changer une roue
change a tire (v)

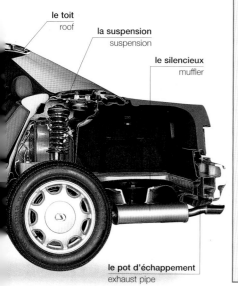

le toit
roof

la suspension
suspension

le silencieux
muffler

le pot d'échappement
exhaust pipe

vocabulaire • vocabulary

l'accident de voiture
car accident

le turbocompresseur
turbocharger

la panne
breakdown

le distributeur
distributor

l'assurance
insurance

le châssis
chassis

la dépanneuse
tow truck

le frein à main
parking brake

le mécanicien *m*
la mécanicienne *f*
mechanic

l'alternateur
alternator

l'arbre à cames
timing belt

la pression des
pneus
tire pressure

le porte-fusibles
fuse box

**Ma voiture est
en panne.**
My car has broken
down.

la bougie
spark plug

la courroie de
ventilateur
fan belt

**Ma voiture ne
démarre pas.**
My car won't start.

le réservoir
d'essence
gas tank

le réglage de
l'allumage
timing

la moto • motorcycle

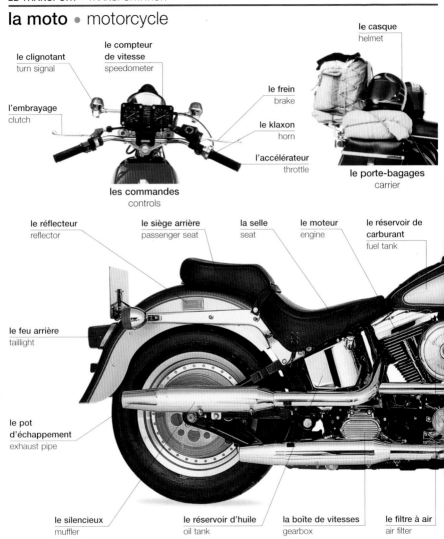

le clignotant
turn signal

le compteur
de vitesse
speedometer

le casque
helmet

le frein
brake

l'embrayage
clutch

le klaxon
horn

l'accélérateur
throttle

le porte-bagages
carrier

les commandes
controls

le réflecteur
reflector

le siège arrière
passenger seat

la selle
seat

le moteur
engine

le réservoir de
carburant
fuel tank

le feu arrière
taillight

le pot
d'échappement
exhaust pipe

le silencieux
muffler

le réservoir d'huile
oil tank

la boîte de vitesses
gearbox

le filtre à air
air filter

les types • types

la visière
visor

le vêtement en cuir
leathers

la bande
fluorescente
reflector strap

la genouillère
knee pad

les vêtements | clothing

le phare
headlight

la suspension
suspension

le garde-boue
fender

la pédale de frein
brake pedal

l'essieu
axle

le pneu
tire

la moto de course | racing bike

le pare-brise
windshield

la moto routière | tourer

la moto tout-terrain | dirt bike

la béquille
stand

le scooter | scooter

le vélo · bicycle

le tandem
tandem

le vélo de course
racing bike

le vélo tout-terrain
(VTT)
mountain bike

la selle
saddle

la tige de selle
seat post

le cadre
frame

la barre
crossbar

la bouteille
d'eau
water bottle

le frein
brake

le moyeu
hub

les vitesses
gears

le casque
helmet

la jante
rim

le pneu
tire

la chaîne
chain

la roue
dentée
cog

la pédale
pedal

la lanière
toe strap

le paracyclisme
paracycle

le vélo pliant
folding bike

la piste cyclable | bike lane

le guidon
handlebar

le levier de vitesse
gear lever

le levier de frein
brake lever

le démonte-pneu
tire lever

la rustine
patch

le kit de réparation | repair kit

la fourche
fork

la clef
key

le rayon
spoke

la pompe
pump

l'antivol
lock

la roue
wheel

la valve
valve

la bande de roulement
tread

la chambre à air
inner tube

le siège d'enfant
child seat

---

vocabulaire • vocabulary

le phare headlight	la béquille kickstand	le patin de frein brake block	le panier basket	le cale-pied toe clip	faire du vélo cycle (v)
le feu arrière rear light	la galerie à vélo bike rack	le câble cable	la dynamo dynamo	pédaler pedal (v)	le vélo électrique electric bike
le cataphote reflector	les stabilisateurs training wheels	le pignon sprocket	la crevaison flat tire	freiner brake (v)	changer de vitesse change gears (v)

le train • train

le numéro
de voie
platform number

le quai
platform

la voie
ferrée
track

la voiture
railcar

le voyageur *m*
la voyageuse *f*
commuter

la gare | train station

les types de trains • types of train

la cabine du
conducteur
engineer's
cab

la locomotive
engine

le rail
rail

le train à vapeur
steam train

le train diesel | diesel train

le train électrique
electric train

le train à grande vitesse
high-speed train

le monorail
monorail

le métro
subway

le tram
tram

le train de marchandises
freight train

le porte-bagages
luggage rack

la fenêtre
window

la porte
door

le siège
seat

le compartiment
compartment

le portillon
ticket gates

le haut-parleur
public address system

l'horaire
schedule

le billet
ticket

la voiture-restaurant
dining car

le hall de gare | concourse

le compartiment-couchettes
sleeping compartment

---

vocabulaire • vocabulary

le réseau ferroviaire railroad network	**le plan de métro** subway map	**le guichet** ticket office	**le rail conducteur** live rail
le TGV express train	**le retard** delay	**le contrôleur** *m* **la contrôleuse** *f* ticket inspector	**le signal** signal
l'heure de pointe rush hour	**le prix** fare	**changer** transfer (v)	**la manette de secours** emergency lever

---

l'avion · aircraft

l'avion de ligne · airliner

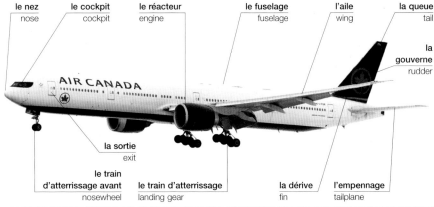

le nez nose	**le cockpit** cockpit	**le réacteur** engine	**le fuselage** fuselage	**l'aile** wing	**la queue** tail

la gouverne
rudder

la sortie
exit

**le train
d'atterrissage avant**
nosewheel

le train d'atterrissage
landing gear

la dérive
fin

l'empennage
tailplane

la cabine · cabin

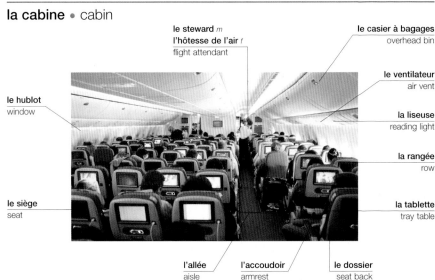

le steward *m*
l'hôtesse de l'air *f*
flight attendant

le casier à bagages
overhead bin

le ventilateur
air vent

le hublot
window

la liseuse
reading light

la rangée
row

le siège
seat

la tablette
tray table

l'allée
aisle

l'accoudoir
armrest

le dossier
seat back

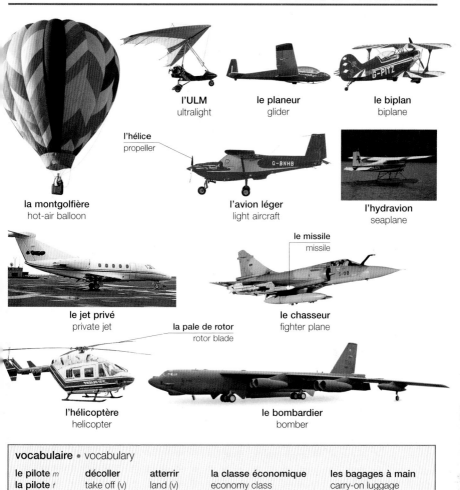

l'ULM
ultralight

le planeur
glider

le biplan
biplane

l'hélice
propeller

la montgolfière
hot-air balloon

l'avion léger
light aircraft

l'hydravion
seaplane

le missile
missile

le jet privé
private jet

le chasseur
fighter plane

la pale de rotor
rotor blade

l'hélicoptère
helicopter

le bombardier
bomber

vocabulaire • vocabulary

le pilote *m*	**décoller**	**atterrir**	**la classe économique**	**les bagages à main**
la pilote *f*	take off (v)	land (v)	economy class	carry-on luggage
pilot				
	voler	**l'altitude**	**la classe affaires**	**la ceinture de sécurité**
le copilote *m*	fly (v)	altitude	business class	seat belt
la copilote *f*				
copilot				

l'aéroport · airport

le tarmac
apron

le véhicule à bagages
baggage trailer

la passerelle
jetway

le véhicule de service
service vehicle

l'avion de ligne | airliner

---

vocabulaire · vocabulary

la piste runway	**la correspondance** connection	**le tapis roulant** baggage carousel	**enregistrer** check in (v)
le terminal terminal	**le numéro de vol** flight number	**la sécurité** security	**la tour de contrôle** control tower
le vol international international flight	**l'immigration** immigration	**la machine de rayons x** X-ray machine	**acheter un billet d'avion** book a flight (v)
le vol intérieur domestic flight	**la douane** customs	**la brochure de vacances** travel brochure	
le comptoir d'enregistrement des bagages baggage drop	**l'excédent de bagages** excess baggage	**les vacances** vacation	

les bagages
à main
carry-on
luggage

le chariot
cart

les bagages
luggage

le numéro
de la porte
d'embarquement
gate number

le visa
visa

le passeport | passport

l'enregistrement des bagages
check-in desk

le contrôle de
passeports
passport control

la carte
d'embarquement
boarding pass

la salle de départ
departure lounge

les départs
departures

les arrivées
arrivals

la destination
destination

l'écran d'information
information screen

le portail électronique de
contrôle des passeports
eGate

la boutique
hors taxes
duty-free shop

le retrait des bagages
baggage claim

la station de taxis
taxi stand

la location
de voitures
car rental

le navire • ship

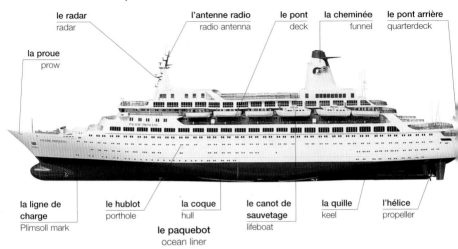

le radar
radar

l'antenne radio
radio antenna

le pont
deck

la cheminée
funnel

le pont arrière
quarterdeck

la proue
prow

la ligne de charge
Plimsoll mark

le hublot
porthole

la coque
hull

le canot de sauvetage
lifeboat

la quille
keel

l'hélice
propeller

le paquebot
ocean liner

la passerelle de commandement
bridge

la salle des moteurs
engine room

la cabine
cabin

la cambuse
galley

vocabulaire • vocabulary

le dock dock	**le guindeau** windlass
le port port	**le runabout** speedboat
la passerelle gangway	**la barque** rowboat
l'ancre anchor	**le canoë** canoe
le bollard bollard	**le capitaine** *m* **la capitaine** *f* captain

autres bateaux · other boats

le ferry
ferry

le moteur
hors-bord
outboard motor

le canot pneumatique
inflatable dinghy

l'hydrofoil
hydrofoil

le yacht
yacht

le catamaran
catamaran

le remorqueur
tugboat

l'aéroglisseur
hovercraft

le navire porte-conteneurs
container ship

la voile
sail

le voilier
sailboat

la cale
hold

le cargo
freighter

le pétrolier
oil tanker

le porte-avions
aircraft carrier

le navire de guerre
battleship

le kiosque
conning tower

le sous-marin
submarine

le port · port

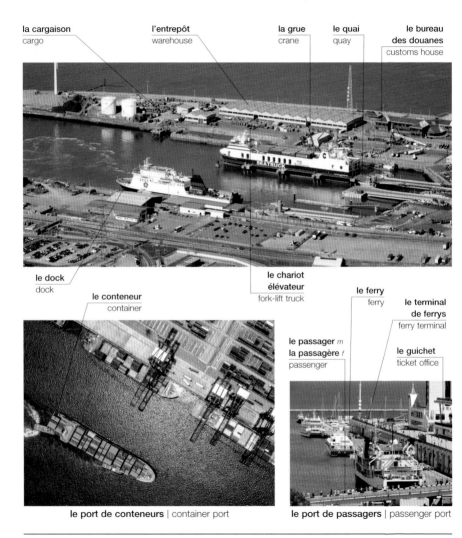

la cargaison
cargo

l'entrepôt
warehouse

la grue
crane

le quai
quay

le bureau
des douanes
customs house

le dock
dock

le chariot
élévateur
fork-lift truck

le ferry
ferry

le terminal
de ferrys
ferry terminal

le conteneur
container

le passager *m*
la passagère *f*
passenger

le guichet
ticket office

le port de conteneurs | container port

le port de passagers | passenger port

le filet
net

le bateau de pêche
fishing boat

les amarres
mooring

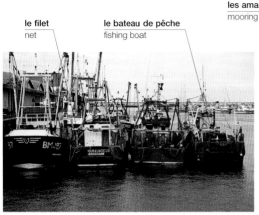

la marina
marina

le port de pêche
fishing port

le port | harbor

l'embarcadère
pier

la jetée
jetty

le chantier naval
shipyard

le feu
lamp

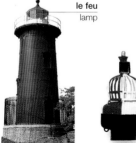

le phare
lighthouse

la bouée
buoy

vocabulaire · vocabulary

le garde-côtes *m*	la cale sèche	embarquer
la garde-côtes *f*	dry dock	board (v)
coast guard		
	mouiller	débarquer
le capitaine de port *m*	moor (v)	disembark (v)
la capitaine de port *f*		
harbor master	se mettre	prendre la mer
	à quai	set sail (v)
jeter l'ancre	dock (v)	
drop anchor (v)		

les sports
sports

le football américain • football

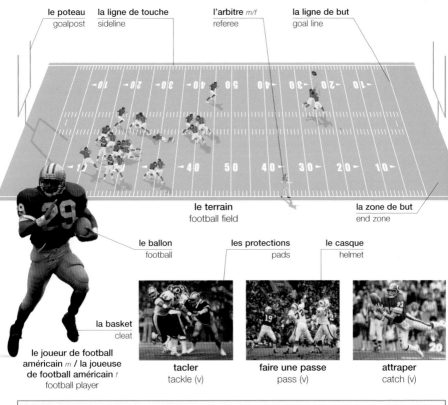

le poteau goalpost	**la ligne de touche** sideline	**l'arbitre** *m/f* referee	**la ligne de but** goal line	

le terrain
football field

la zone de but
end zone

le ballon
football

les protections
pads

le casque
helmet

la basket
cleat

le joueur de football américain *m* / **la joueuse de football américain** *f*
football player

tacler
tackle (v)

faire une passe
pass (v)

attraper
catch (v)

---

vocabulaire • vocabulary

le temps mort time out	**l'équipe** team	**la défense** defense	**le but** touchdown	**Où en est le match?** What is the score?
la perte de ballon fumble	**l'attaque** attack	**le score** score	**le meneur de claque** *m* **la meneuse de claque** *f* cheerleader	**Qui est-ce qui gagne?** Who is winning?

---

le rugby • rugby

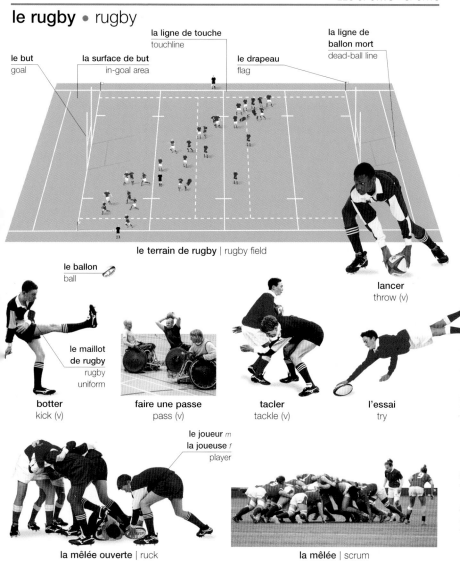

la ligne de touche
touchline

la ligne de
ballon mort
dead-ball line

le but
goal

la surface de but
in-goal area

le drapeau
flag

le terrain de rugby | rugby field

le ballon
ball

lancer
throw (v)

le maillot
de rugby
rugby
uniform

botter
kick (v)

faire une passe
pass (v)

tacler
tackle (v)

l'essai
try

le joueur *m*
la joueuse *f*
player

la mêlée ouverte | ruck

la mêlée | scrum

le football • soccer

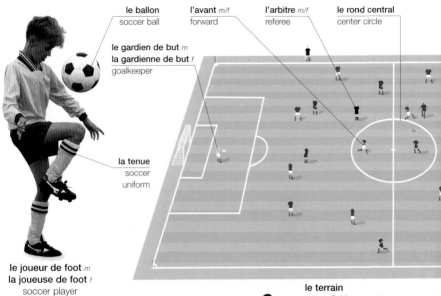

le ballon
soccer ball

l'avant *m/f*
forward

l'arbitre *m/f*
referee

le rond central
center circle

le gardien de but *m*
la gardienne de but *f*
goalkeeper

la tenue
soccer
uniform

le joueur de foot *m*
la joueuse de foot *f*
soccer player

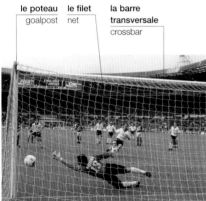

le poteau
goalpost

le filet
net

la barre
transversale
crossbar

le but | goal

le terrain
soccer field

dribbler | dribble (v)

faire une tête
head (v)

le mur
wall

le coup franc | free kick

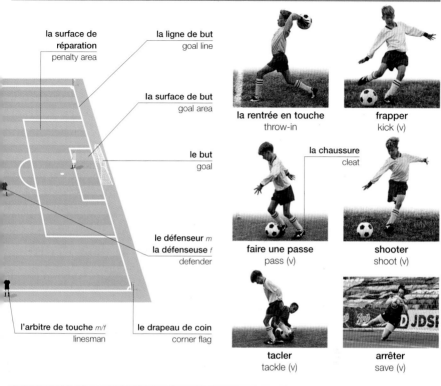

la surface de
réparation
penalty area

la ligne de but
goal line

la surface de but
goal area

le but
goal

le défenseur *m*
la défenseuse *f*
defender

l'arbitre de touche *m/f*
linesman

le drapeau de coin
corner flag

la rentrée en touche
throw-in

frapper
kick (v)

la chaussure
cleat

faire une passe
pass (v)

shooter
shoot (v)

tacler
tackle (v)

arrêter
save (v)

vocabulaire • vocabulary

le stade stadium	**la faute** foul	**le carton jaune** yellow card	**le championnat** league	**la prolongation** extra time
marquer un but score a goal (v)	**le corner** corner	**l'hors-jeu** offside	**le match nul** tie	**le remplacement** substitution
le penalty penalty	**le carton rouge** red card	**l'exclusion** send off	**la mi-temps** half-time	**le remplaçant** *m* **la remplaçante** *f* substitute

le hockey • hockey

le hockey sur glace • ice hockey

la zone de défense
defending zone

la ligne de but
goal line

la zone
d'attaque
attack zone

la zone neutre
neutral zone

le gardien de but *m*
la gardienne de but *f*
goalkeeper

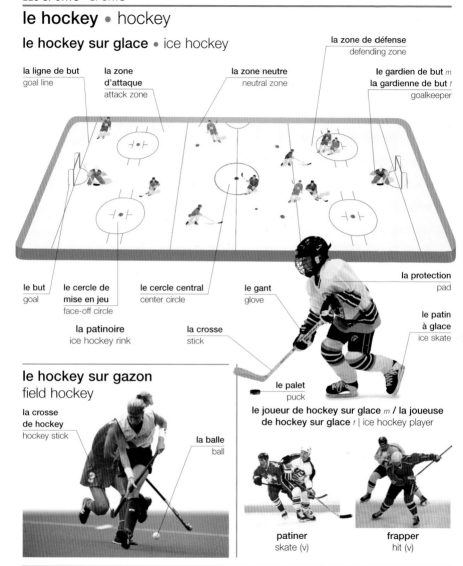

le but
goal

le cercle de
mise en jeu
face-off circle

le cercle central
center circle

le gant
glove

la protection
pad

le patin
à glace
ice skate

la patinoire
ice hockey rink

la crosse
stick

le palet
puck

le joueur de hockey sur glace *m* / la joueuse
de hockey sur glace *f* | ice hockey player

le hockey sur gazon
field hockey

la crosse
de hockey
hockey stick

la balle
ball

patiner
skate (v)

frapper
hit (v)

le cricket • cricket

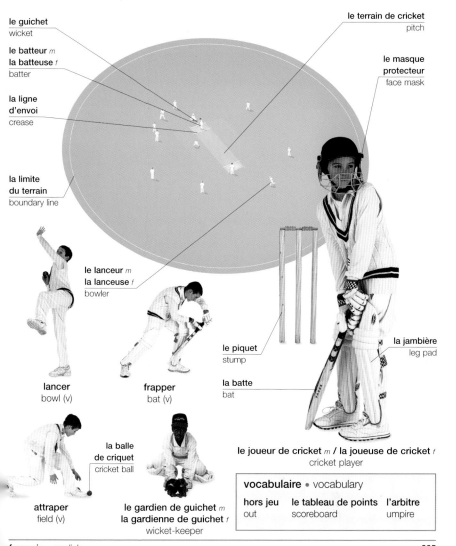

le guichet
wicket

le batteur *m*
la batteuse *f*
batter

la ligne
d'envoi
crease

la limite
du terrain
boundary line

le terrain de cricket
pitch

le masque
protecteur
face mask

le lanceur *m*
la lanceuse *f*
bowler

lancer
bowl (v)

frapper
bat (v)

le piquet
stump

la batte
bat

la jambière
leg pad

attraper
field (v)

la balle
de criquet
cricket ball

le gardien de guichet *m*
la gardienne de guichet *f*
wicket-keeper

le joueur de cricket *m* / la joueuse de cricket *f*
cricket player

vocabulaire • vocabulary

hors jeu	le tableau de points	l'arbitre
out	scoreboard	umpire

le basket • basketball

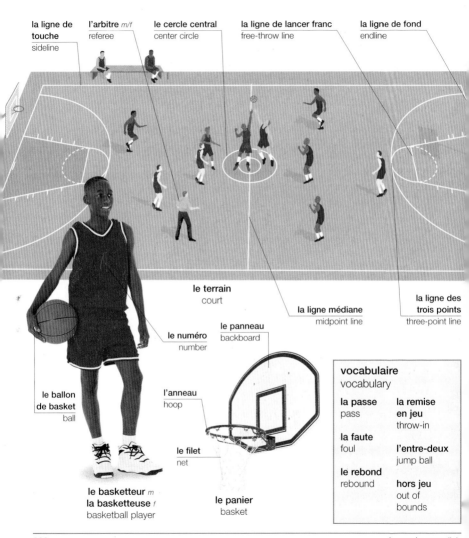

la ligne de touche
sideline

l'arbitre *m/f*
referee

le cercle central
center circle

la ligne de lancer franc
free-throw line

la ligne de fond
endline

le terrain
court

la ligne médiane
midpoint line

la ligne des trois points
three-point line

le numéro
number

le panneau
backboard

le ballon de basket
ball

l'anneau
hoop

le filet
net

le basketteur *m*
la basketteuse *f*
basketball player

le panier
basket

vocabulaire
vocabulary

la passe pass	la remise en jeu throw-in
la faute foul	l'entre-deux jump ball
le rebond rebound	hors jeu out of bounds

les actions • actions

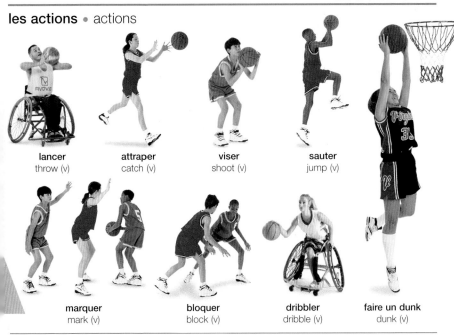

lancer	attraper	viser	sauter
throw (v)	catch (v)	shoot (v)	jump (v)

marquer	bloquer	dribbler	faire un dunk
mark (v)	block (v)	dribble (v)	dunk (v)

le volley • volleyball

bloquer
block (v)

le filet
net

**faire une
manchette**
dig (v)

l'arbitre *m/f*
referee

la genouillère
knee support

le terrain | court

le baseball • baseball

le terrain • field

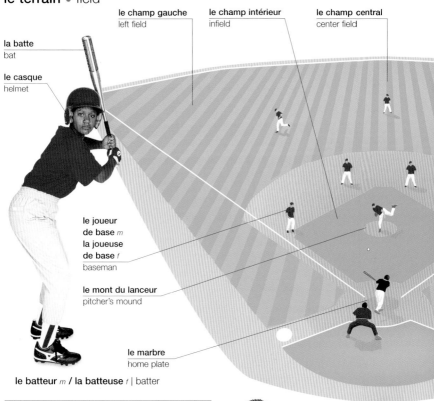

le champ gauche
left field

le champ intérieur
infield

le champ central
center field

la batte
bat

le casque
helmet

le joueur
de base *m*
la joueuse
de base *f*
baseman

le mont du lanceur
pitcher's mound

le marbre
home plate

le batteur *m* **/ la batteuse** *f* | batter

vocabulaire • vocabulary

le tour de batte inning	**sauf** *m* **sauve** *f* safe	**la fausse balle** foul ball
le point run	**hors jeu** out	**la prise** strike

la balle
ball

le gant
glove

le masque
mask

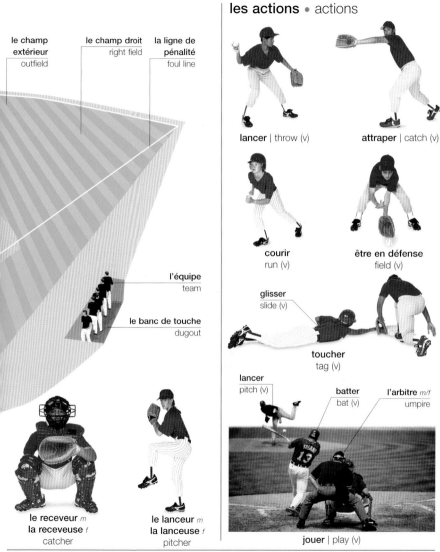

les actions • actions

le champ
extérieur
outfield

le champ droit
right field

la ligne de
pénalité
foul line

l'équipe
team

le banc de touche
dugout

lancer | throw (v)

attraper | catch (v)

courir
run (v)

être en défense
field (v)

glisser
slide (v)

toucher
tag (v)

lancer
pitch (v)

batter
bat (v)

l'arbitre *m/f*
umpire

jouer | play (v)

le receveur *m*
la receveuse *f*
catcher

le lanceur *m*
la lanceuse *f*
pitcher

le tennis • tennis

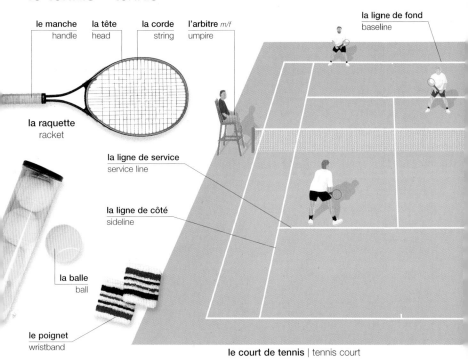

le manche handle	**la tête** head	**la corde** string	**l'arbitre** *m/f* umpire

la ligne de fond baseline

la raquette racket

la ligne de service service line

la ligne de côté sideline

la balle ball

le poignet wristband

le court de tennis | tennis court

---

vocabulaire • vocabulary

le simple singles	**le set** set	**l'égalité** deuce	**la faute** fault	**le slice** slice	**l'effet** spin
le double doubles	**le match** match	**l'avantage** advantage	**l'as** ace	**l'échange** rally	**l'arbitre de ligne** *m/f* linesman
le jeu game	**le tiebreak** tiebreaker	**zéro** love	**l'amorti** drop shot	**net!** let!	**le championnat** championship

les coups • strokes

le filet
net

le smash
smash

le ramasseur
de balles *m*
la ramasseuse
de balles *f*
ball boy / ball girl

servir
serve (v)

les tennis
tennis shoes

le joueur de tennis *m*
la joueuse de tennis *f*
player

le service
serve

la volée
volley

le retour
return

le lob
lob

le coup droit
forehand

le revers
backhand

les jeux de raquette • racket games

le volant
shuttlecock

la raquette
paddle

le badminton
badminton

le tennis de table
table tennis

le squash
squash

le racquetball
racquetball

le golf • golf

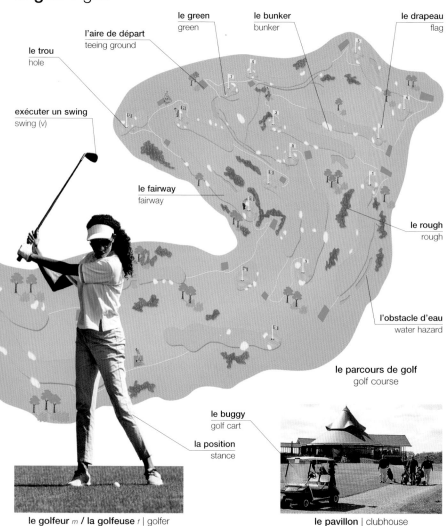

le green
green

le bunker
bunker

le drapeau
flag

l'aire de départ
teeing ground

le trou
hole

exécuter un swing
swing (v)

le fairway
fairway

le rough
rough

l'obstacle d'eau
water hazard

le parcours de golf
golf course

le buggy
golf cart

la position
stance

le golfeur *m* / la golfeuse *f* | golfer

le pavillon | clubhouse

l'équipement • equipment

la balle de golf
golf ball

le tee
tee

le sac de golf
golf bag

les pointes
spikes

le gant
glove

le caddie
bag cart

la chaussure de golf
golf shoe

les clubs de golf
golf clubs

le bois
wood

le putter
putter

le fer
iron

le wedge
wedge

les actions • actions

partir du tee
tee off (v)

driver
drive (v)

putter
putt (v)

faire un chip
chip (v)

---

vocabulaire • vocabulary

le par par	au-dessus du par over par	le handicap handicap	le caddie caddy	le backswing backswing	le coup stroke
en dessous du par under par	le trou en un hole in one	le tournoi tournament	les spectateurs spectators	le swing d'essai practice swing	la ligne de jeu line of play

l'athlétisme • track and field

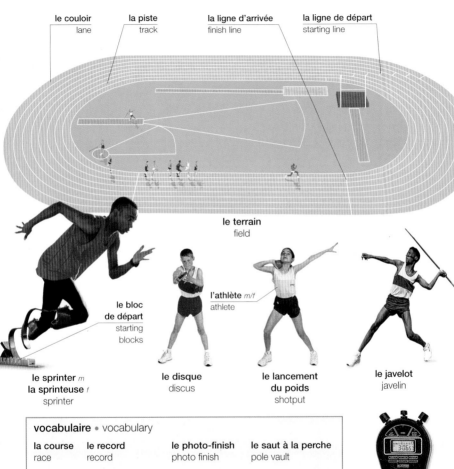

le couloir
lane

la piste
track

la ligne d'arrivée
finish line

la ligne de départ
starting line

le terrain
field

le bloc
de départ
starting
blocks

l'athlète *m/f*
athlete

le sprinter *m*
la sprinteuse *f*
sprinter

le disque
discus

le lancement
du poids
shotput

le javelot
javelin

---

vocabulaire • vocabulary

la course race	le record record	le photo-finish photo finish	le saut à la perche pole vault
le temps time	battre un record break a record (v)	le marathon marathon	le record personnel personal best

le chronomètre
stopwatch

le bâton
baton

la barre
crossbar

la course de relais
relay race

le saut en hauteur
high jump

le saut en longueur
long jump

la course de haies
hurdles

la gymnastique • gymnastics

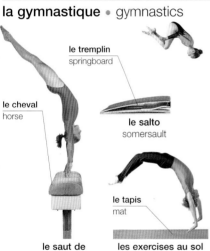

le tremplin
springboard

le gymnaste *m*
la gymnaste *f*
gymnast

le cheval
horse

le salto
somersault

la poutre
balance beam

le ruban
ribbon

le tapis
mat

**le saut de
cheval**
vault

les exercises au sol
floor exercises

la roue
cartwheel

**la gymnastique
rythmique**
rhythmic gymnastics

---

vocabulaire • vocabulary

la barre fixe horizontal bar	**le cheval d'arçons** pommel horse	**les anneaux** rings	**les médailles** medals	**l'argent** silver
les barres parallèles parallel bars	**les barres asymétriques** asymmetric bars	**le podium** podium	**l'or** gold	**le bronze** bronze

---

les sports de combat • combat sports

le protège-tête
guard

le gant
glove

l'adversaire *m/f*
opponent

la ceinture
belt

le taekwondo
tae kwon do

le masque
mask

le sabre
sword

le karaté
karate

le judo
judo

le kung-fu
kung fu

l'aïkido
aikido

le kendo
kendo

le kickboxing
kickboxing

la lutte
wrestling

la boxe
boxing

les actions • actions

la chute
fall

la prise
hold

la projection
throw

l'immobilisation
pin

le coup de pied
kick

le coup de poing
punch

le coup
strike

le saut
jump

le blocage
block

le coup
chop

---

vocabulaire • vocabulary

le ring boxing ring	**le round** round	**le poing** fist	**la ceinture noire** black belt	**la capoeira** capoeira
les gants de boxe boxing gloves	**le combat** bout	**le K.-O.** knockout	**l'autodéfense** self-defense	**le sumo** sumo wrestling
le protège-dents mouth guard	**l'entraînement** sparring	**le punching-ball** punching bag	**les arts martiaux** martial arts	**le taï chi** tai chi

la natation • swimming

l'équipement • equipment

le pince-nez
nose clip

la brassière
water wings

les lunettes protectrices
goggles

la planche
kickboard

le maillot de bain
swimsuit

le couloir
lane

**le bonnet
de natation**
swimming
cap

l'eau
water

**le plot
de départ**
starting block

**le slip
de bain**
swim briefs

la piscine
swimming pool

le nageur *m* / **la nageuse** *f*
swimmer

le tremplin
diving board

le plongeur *m* / **la plongeuse** *f*
diver

plonger | dive (v)

nager | swim (v)

le virage-culbute | turn

les styles • styles

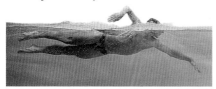

le **crawl** | front crawl

la **brasse** | breaststroke

la **nage**
stroke

le **coup de pied**
kick

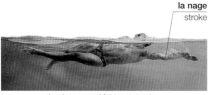

le **dos crawlé** | backstroke

le **papillon** | butterfly

la plongée • scuba diving

la **combinaison
de plongée**
wetsuit

la **palme**
fin

la **ceinture
de plomb**
weight belt

la **bouteille d'air**
air tank

le **masque**
mask

le **régulateur**
regulator

le **tuba**
snorkel

vocabulaire • vocabulary

le **plongeon** dive	le **départ plongé** racing dive	le **maître-nageur** *m* la **maître-nageuse** *f* lifeguard	le **grand bassin** deep end	la **nage synchronisée** synchronized swimming	**nager sur place** tread water (v)
le **plongeon de haut vol** high dive	les **casiers** lockers	le **water-polo** water polo	le **petit bassin** shallow end	la **crampe** cramp	**se noyer** drown (v)

la voile • sailing

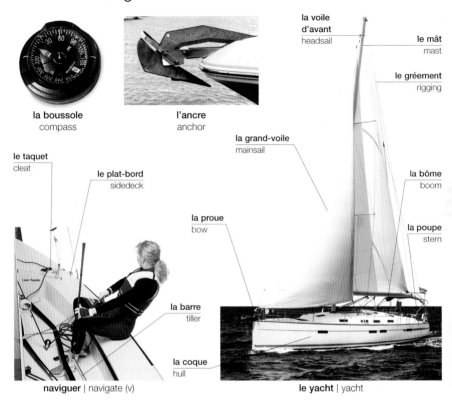

la boussole
compass

l'ancre
anchor

la voile
d'avant
headsail

le mât
mast

le gréement
rigging

la grand-voile
mainsail

la bôme
boom

le taquet
cleat

le plat-bord
sidedeck

la poupe
stern

la proue
bow

la barre
tiller

la coque
hull

naviguer | navigate (v)

le yacht | yacht

la sécurité • safety

la fusée éclairante
flare

la bouée de sauvetage
life buoy

le gilet de sauvetage
life jacket

le radeau de sauvetage
life raft

les sports aquatiques • watersports

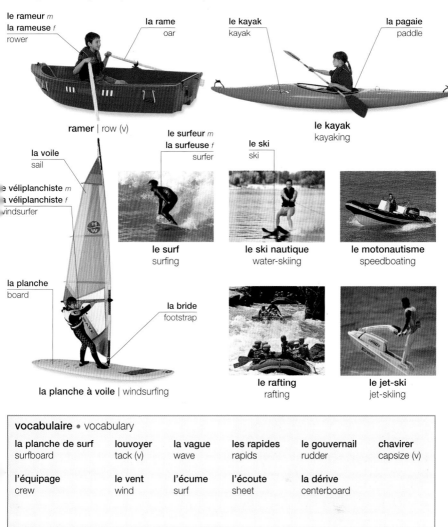

le rameur *m*
la rameuse *f*
rower

la rame
oar

le kayak
kayak

la pagaie
paddle

ramer | row (v)

le kayak
kayaking

la voile
sail

le surfeur *m*
la surfeuse *f*
surfer

le ski
ski

le véliplanchiste *m*
la véliplanchiste *f*
windsurfer

le surf
surfing

le ski nautique
water-skiing

le motonautisme
speedboating

la planche
board

la bride
footstrap

la planche à voile | windsurfing

le rafting
rafting

le jet-ski
jet-skiing

vocabulaire • vocabulary

la planche de surf surfboard	louvoyer tack (v)	la vague wave	les rapides rapids	le gouvernail rudder	chavirer capsize (v)
l'équipage crew	le vent wind	l'écume surf	l'écoute sheet	la dérive centerboard	

l'équitation • horseback riding

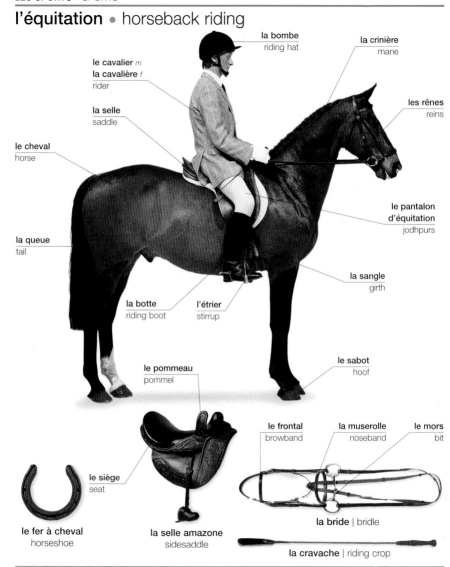

la bombe
riding hat

la crinière
mane

le cavalier *m*
la cavalière *f*
rider

les rênes
reins

la selle
saddle

le cheval
horse

le pantalon d'équitation
jodhpurs

la queue
tail

la sangle
girth

la botte
riding boot

l'étrier
stirrup

le sabot
hoof

le pommeau
pommel

le frontal
browband

la muserolle
noseband

le mors
bit

le siège
seat

la bride | bridle

le fer à cheval
horseshoe

la selle amazone
sidesaddle

la cravache | riding crop

les courses • events

le cheval de course
racehorse

l'obstacle
fence

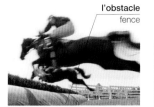

la course de chevaux
horse race

le steeple-chase
steeplechase

la course de trot attelé
harness race

le rodéo
rodeo

le jumping
showjumping

la course attelée
carriage race

la randonnée
trail riding

le dressage
dressage

le polo
polo

---

vocabulaire • vocabulary

le pas walk	**le petit galop** canter	**le saut** jump	**le licol** halter	**l'enclos** paddock	**la course de plat** flat race
le trot trot	**le galop** gallop	**le palefrenier** m **la palefrenière** f groom	**l'écurie** stable	**l'arène** arena	**l'hippodrome** racecourse

---

la pêche • fishing

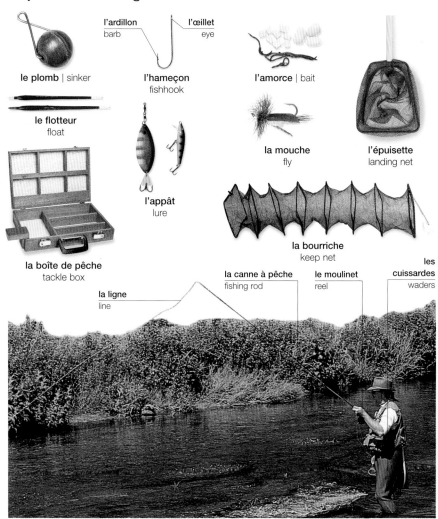

le plomb | sinker

l'ardillon
barb

l'œillet
eye

l'hameçon
fishhook

l'amorce | bait

le flotteur
float

l'appât
lure

la mouche
fly

l'épuisette
landing net

la boîte de pêche
tackle box

la bourriche
keep net

la ligne
line

la canne à pêche
fishing rod

le moulinet
reel

les cuissardes
waders

le pêcheur à la ligne *m* / **la pêcheuse à la ligne** *f* | angler

les genres de pêche • types of fishing

la pêche en eau douce
freshwater fishing

la pêche à la mouche
fly-fishing

la pêche sportive
sportfishing

la pêche hauturière
deep-sea fishing

la pêche au lancer en mer
surfcasting

les activités • activities

lancer
cast (v)

attraper
catch (v)

ramener
reel in (v)

prendre au filet
net (v)

lâcher
release (v)

---

vocabulaire • vocabulary

amorcer bait (v)	**le matériel de pêche** tackle	**les vêtements imperméables** rain gear	**le permis de pêche** fishing license	**le panier de pêche** creel
mordre bite (v)	**le tambour** spool	**la perche** pole	**la pêche maritime** marine fishing	**la pêche sous-marine** spearfishing

---

le ski • skiing

la pente de ski
ski slope

le télésiège
chairlift

la télécabine
cable car

la piste de ski
ski run

le bâton
de ski
ski pole

le gant
glove

la barrière
de sécurité
safety barrier

la spatule
tip

la carre
edge

le ski
ski

la veste de ski
ski jacket

le skieur *m* / la skieuse *f*
skier

la chaussure de ski
ski boot

les épreuves • events

la descente
downhill skiing

la porte
gate

le slalom
slalom

le saut
ski jump

le ski de fond
cross-country skiing

les sports d'hiver • winter sports

l'escalade sur glace
ice climbing

le patin à glace
ice-skating

les lunettes
de ski
goggles

le patin
à glace
skate

le patinage artistique
figure skating

le snowboard
snowboarding

le bobsleigh
bobsled

la luge
luge

la motoneige
snowmobile

la luge
sledding

vocabulaire • vocabulary

le ski alpin alpine skiing	**le curling** curling
le slalom géant giant slalom	**le patinage de vitesse** speed skating
hors piste off-piste	**le biathlon** biathlon
le mushing dogsledding	**l'avalanche** avalanche

les autres sports • other sports

le planeur
glider

le deltaplane
hang-glider

le planeur
gliding

le parachute
parachute

le deltaplane
hang-gliding

la corde
rope

l'escalade
rock climbing

le parachutisme
parachuting

le parapente
paragliding

le saut en parachute
skydiving

le rappel
rappelling

le saut à l'élastique
bungee jumping

le pilote
automobile *m*
la pilote
automobile *f*
race-car driver

le rallye
rally driving

la course automobile
auto racing

le motocross
motocross

la course de moto
motorcycle racing

la planche à
roulettes
skateboard

la crosse
stick

le
masque
mask

le
fleuret
foil

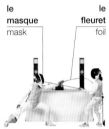

le skateboard
skateboarding

le roller
inline skating

le lacrosse
lacrosse

l'escrime
fencing

la quille
pin

l'arc
bow

la cible
target

la flèche
arrow

le carquois
quiver

le tir à l'arc
archery

le tir sportif
target shooting

la boule
de bowling
bowling ball

le bowling
bowling

le billard américain
pool

le billard
snooker

la forme physique • fitness

le vélo d'entraînement
exercise bike

l'appareil de musculation
gym machine

le banc
bench

les poids
free weights

la barre
bar

la salle de sport
gym

la machine
à ramer
rowing machine

le tapis de course
treadmill

le vélo elliptique
elliptical trainer

le coach personnel *m*
la coach personnelle *f*
personal trainer

le stepper
stair machine

la piscine
swimming pool

le sauna
sauna

les exercices • exercises

l'étirement
stretch

la fente en avant
lunge

la pompe
push-up

le squat
squat

les abdominaux
sit-up

l'haltère
dumbbell

les flexions de biceps
bicep curl

la presse à cuisse
leg press

la presse à pectoraux
chest press

la barre à poids
weight bar

les baskets
sneakers

l'entraînement poids et haltères
weight training

le jogging
jogging

le Pilates
Pilates

---

vocabulaire • vocabulary

s'entraîner train (v)	**jogger sur place** jog in place (v)	**étendre** extend (v)	**les exercices de boxe** boxercise	**le circuit training** circuit training
s'échauffer warm up (v)	**fléchir** flex (v)	**tirer** pull up (v)	**le saut à la corde** jumping rope	**le vélo fitness** spin class

---

le temps libre
leisure

le théâtre • theater

le rideau
curtain

les coulisses
wings

le décor
set

le public
audience

l'orchestre
orchestra

la scène | stage

le fauteuil
seat

la deuxième galerie
balcony seats

la rangée
row

la loge
box

la corbeille
mezzanine

le balcon
balcony

l'allée
aisle

l'orchestre
orchestra
seats

les places | seating

vocabulaire • vocabulary

la distribution cast	**le fond de scène** backdrop	**la première** opening night
l'acteur *m* **l'actrice** *f* actor	**le metteur en scène** *m* **la metteuse en scène** *f* director	**l'entracte** intermission
la pièce de théâtre play		**le programme** program
le texte script	**le producteur** *m* **la productrice** *f* producer	**la fosse d'orchestre** orchestra pit

le concert
concert

la comédie musicale
musical

le costume
costume

le ballet
ballet

vocabulaire • vocabulary

la musique classique
classical music

applaudir
applaud (v)

la partition
musical score

le rappel
encore

la bande sonore
soundtrack

l'ouvreur *m*
l'ouvreuse *f*
usher

Ça commence à quelle heure?
What time does it start?

Je voudrais deux billets pour la représentation de ce soir.
I'd like two tickets for tonight's performance.

l'opéra
opera

le cinéma • movies

le pop-corn
popcorn

le foyer
lobby

la caisse
box office

l'affiche
poster

le cinéma
movie theater

l'écran
screen

vocabulaire • vocabulary

la comédie
comedy

la comédie romantique
romance

le thriller
thriller

le film de science-fiction
science fiction movie

le film d'horreur
horror movie

le film d'aventures
adventure movie

le western
western

le film d'animation
animated movie

l'orchestre • orchestra

les cordes • strings

la harpe
harp

le chef d'orchestre *m*
la cheffe d'orchestre *f*
conductor

la contrebasse
double bass

le violon
violin

le podium
podium

le violoncelle
cello

l'alto
viola

la partition
score

la clé de sol
treble clef

la note
note

la portée
staff

la clé de fa
bass clef

la notation | notation

le piano | piano

---

vocabulaire • vocabulary

l'ouverture overture	**la sonate** sonata	**le silence** rest	**le dièse** sharp	**le bécarre** natural	**la gamme** scale
la symphonie symphony	**les instruments** instruments	**le ton** pitch	**le bémol** flat	**la barre de mesure** bar	**la baguette** baton

les bois • woodwind

le piccolo
piccolo

la flûte traversière
flute

le hautbois
oboe

le cor anglais
English horn

la clarinette
clarinet

la clarinette basse
bass clarinet

le basson
bassoon

le contrebasson
double bassoon

le saxophone
saxophone

les percussions • percussion

le vibraphone
vibraphone

les bongos
bongos

la caisse claire
snare drum

la timbale
kettledrum

le gong
gong

le triangle
triangle

les maracas
maracas

les cymbales
cymbals

le tambour
tambourine

la pédale
foot pedal

les cuivres • brass

la trompette
trumpet

le trombone
trombone

le cor
French horn

le tuba
tuba

le concert • concert

le haut-parleur
speaker

le chanteur *m*
la chanteuse *f*
lead singer

le guitariste *m*
la guitariste *f*
guitarist

le microphone
microphone

le batteur *m*
la batteuse *f*
drummer

les fans
fans

le concert de rock | rock concert

les instruments • instruments

le micro
pickup

le manche
neck

la frette
fret

la cheville
tuning peg

la corde
string

le chevalet
bridge

le tambour
drum

la basse
bass guitar

le clavier
keyboard

la guitare électrique
electric guitar

la batterie
drum kit

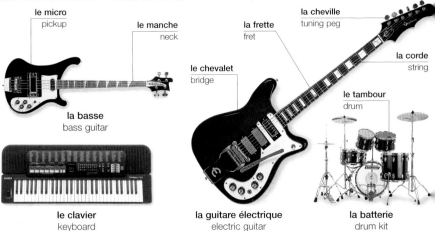

les styles de musique • musical styles

le jazz
jazz

le blues
blues

le gospel
gospel

la musique folk
folk music

la pop
pop

la danse
dance music

le rap
rap

le heavy métal
heavy metal

la musique classique
classical music

---

vocabulaire • vocabulary

la chanson	**les paroles**	**la mélodie**	**le rythme**	**le reggae**	**la country**	**le projecteur**
song	lyrics	melody	beat	reggae	country	spotlight

---

le tourisme • sightseeing

le touriste *m*
la touriste *f*
tourist

l'itinéraire
itinerary

à impériale
open-top

le bus touristique | tour bus

l'attraction touristique | tourist attraction

le guide touristique *m*
la guide touristique *f*
tour guide

la statuette
figurine

la visite guidée
guided tour

les souvenirs
souvenirs

---

vocabulaire • vocabulary

ouvert *m* **ouverte** *f* open	**le guide** guidebook	**l'appareil photo** camera	**à droite** right	**Où est… ?** Where is… ?
fermé *m* **fermée** *f* closed	**les piles** batteries	**les directions** directions	**tout droit** straight ahead	**Je me suis perdu.** I'm lost.
le prix d'entrée entrance fee	**l'audioguide** audioguide	**à gauche** left		**Pour aller à…, s'il vous plaît?** Can you tell me the way to… ?

---

les attractions • attractions

le tableau
painting

l'œuvre
exhibit

le musée d'art
art gallery

la statue
statue

le monument
monument

l'exposition
exhibition

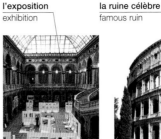

le musée
museum

la ruine célèbre
famous ruin

**le monument
historique**
historic building

le casino
casino

le parc
gardens

le parc national
national park

l'information • information

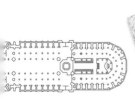

le plan de niveau
floor plan

le plan
map

les heures
times

l'horaire
schedule

**les informations
touristiques**
tourist information

les activités de plein air • outdoor activities

le sentier
footpath

le cadran solaire
sundial

le café
café

le parc | park

la pelouse
grass

le banc
bench

les jardins à
la française
formal gardens

les montagnes
russes
roller coaster

la fête foraine
fairground

le parc d'attractions
theme park

la réserve
safari park

le zoo
zoo

les activités • activities

le vélo
cycling

le jogging
jogging

le skateboard
skateboarding

le roller
rollerblading

la piste cavalière
bridle path

**l'observation
des oiseaux**
bird-watching

l'équitation
horseback riding

la randonnée
hiking

**le panier à
pique-nique**
picnic basket

le pique-nique
picnic

le terrain de jeux • playground

le bac à sable
sandbox

la pataugeoire
wading pool

la balançoire
swing

la bascule | seesaw

le toboggan
slide

la cage à poules
climbing frame

la plage • beach

l'hôtel
hotel

le parasol
beach umbrella

la vague
wave

la mer
sea

le sable
sand

la chaise longue
sun lounger

le short de bain
swimming briefs

le sac de plage
beach bag

le bikini
bikini

faire bronzette | sunbathe (v)

le sauveteur *m*
la sauveteuse *f*
lifeguard

le poste de secours
lifeguard tower

le pare-vent
windbreak

la promenade
boardwalk

le transat
deck chair

les lunettes de soleil
sunglasses

le chapeau de plage
sun hat

la crème solaire
suntan lotion

l'écran total
sunscreen

le ballon de plage
beach ball

la bouée
inflatable ring

le maillot de bain
swimsuit

la pelle
shovel

le seau
pail

le château de sable
sandcastle

le coquillage
shell

la serviette de plage
beach towel

le camping • camping

les poubelles
waste disposal

les toilettes
restrooms

les sanitaires
shower block

le branchement électrique
electric hookup

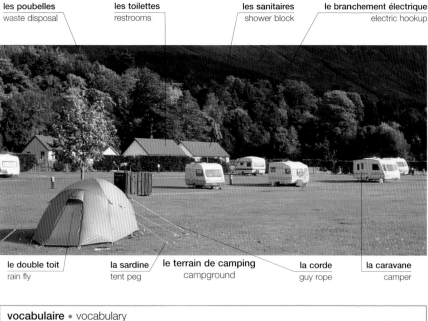

le double toit
rain fly

la sardine
tent peg

le terrain de camping
campground

la corde
guy rope

la caravane
camper

vocabulaire • vocabulary

camper
camp (v)

l'emplacement
site

le banc à pique-nique
picnic bench

le charbon de bois
charcoal

l'accueil
site manager's office

monter une tente
pitch a tent (v)

le hamac
hammock

l'allume-feu
firelighter

les emplacements libres
sites available

le mât
tent pole

le camping-car
camper van

allumer un feu
light a fire (v)

complet
full

le lit de camp
camp bed

la remorque
trailer

le feu de camp
campfire

le cadre
frame

le tapis de sol
ground sheet

le sac à dos
backpack

le thermos
vacuum flask

la bouteille d'eau
water bottle

la tente
tent

le répulsif
insect repellent

la lampe torche
flashlight

la moustiquaire
mosquito net

les sous-vêtements
thermiques
thermal underwear

les chaussures
de marche
hiking boots

les vêtements
imperméables
rain gear

le sac de couchage
sleeping bag

le réchaud
camping stove

le barbecue
barbecue grill

le tapis de sol
sleeping mat

le matelas pneumatique | air mattress

les loisirs électroniques • home entertainment

la télévision à écran plat
flatscreen TV

l'amplificateur
amplifier

le baffle
speaker

le support
speaker stand

le retour
rapide
rewind

l'avance rapide
fast-forward

le volume
volume

la lecture
play

la pause
pause

l'enregistrement
record

l'arrêt
stop

la télécommande
remote control

le lecteur DVD
DVD player

la station de charge
dock

le boîtier TV
DTV converter box

la radio numérique
digital radio

l'antenne parabolique
satellite dish

le viseur
eyecup

l'écran
screen

le caméscope
camcorder

la console
console

la manette
controller

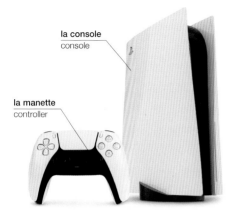

le jeu vidéo | video game

l'enceinte connectée
smart speaker

l'étui
case

l'enceinte Bluetooth
bluetooth speaker

les écouteurs
headphones

les écouteurs sans fil
wireless earphones

---

vocabulaire • vocabulary

le film
feature film

le karaoké
karaoke

le lecteur CD
CD player

la publicité
advertisement

numérique
digital

le téléviseur connecté
smart TV

le streaming
streaming

le wifi
Wi-Fi

le programme
program

la barre de son
soundbar

stéréo
stereo

la haute définition
high-definition

la télévision par câble
cable television

la chaîne payante
change channel (v)

allumer la télévision
turn on the television (v)

regarder la télévision
watch television (v)

éteindre la télévision
turn off the television (v)

---

la photographie • photography

le déclencheur
shutter release

le réglage
de l'ouverture
aperture dial

l'objectif
lens

l'appareil réflex mono-objectif | SLR camera

le filtre
filter

le bouchon d'objectif
lens cap

le flash compact
flash gun

le posemètre
lightmeter

le zoom
zoom lens

le trépied
tripod

les types d'appareils photo • types of camera

le Polaroid®
Polaroid camera

le flash
flash

l'appareil numérique
digital camera

le photophone
camera phone

l'appareil jetable
disposable camera

photographier • photograph (v)

mettre au point
focus (v)

développer
develop (v)

le négatif
negative

le selfie
selfie

paysage
landscape

portrait
portrait

la photo | photograph

l'album de photos
photo album

le cadre de photo
picture frame

les problèmes • problems

sous-exposé
underexposed

surexposé
overexposed

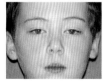

flou
out of focus

les yeux rouges
red eye

vocabulaire • vocabulary

le viseur
viewfinder

l'épreuve
print

le sac d'appareil photo
camera case

mat
matte

la pose
exposure

brilliant
gloss

la pellicule
film

l'agrandissement
enlargement

**Pourriez-vous faire développer
cette pellicule?**
I'd like this film processed.

les jeux • games

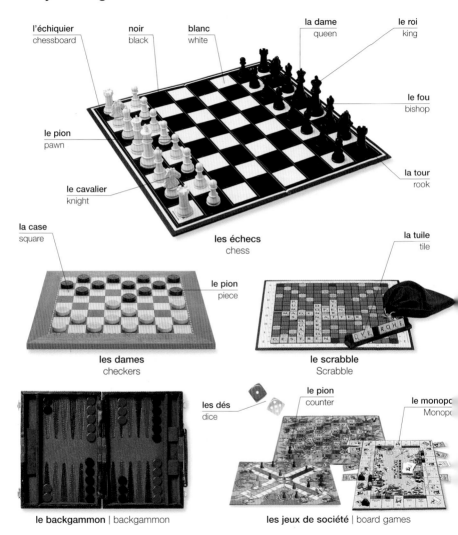

l'échiquier
chessboard

noir
black

blanc
white

la dame
queen

le roi
king

le fou
bishop

le pion
pawn

la tour
rook

le cavalier
knight

la case
square

les échecs
chess

le pion
piece

la tuile
tile

les dames
checkers

le scrabble
Scrabble

les dés
dice

le pion
counter

le monopc
Monopc

le backgammon | backgammon

les jeux de société | board games

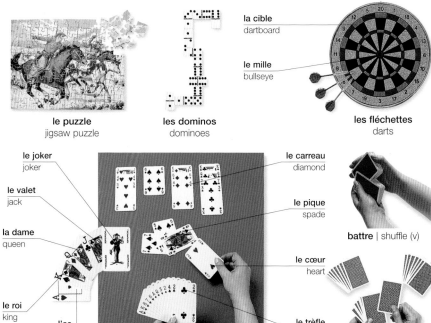

la cible
dartboard

le mille
bullseye

le puzzle
jigsaw puzzle

les dominos
dominoes

les fléchettes
darts

le joker
joker

le carreau
diamond

le valet
jack

le pique
spade

la dame
queen

battre | shuffle (v)

le cœur
heart

le roi
king

l'as
ace

le trèfle
club

les cartes
cards

distribuer | deal (v)

---

vocabulaire • vocabulary

jouer play (v)	**gagner** win (v)	**perdre** lose (v)	**le point** point	**le bridge** bridge	**Jette le dé.** Roll the dice.
le joueur *m* **la joueuse** *f* player	**le gagnant** *m* **la gagnante** *f* winner	**le perdant** *m* **la perdante** *f* loser	**le score** score **le poker** poker	**le jeu de cartes** deck of cards **la couleur** suit	**C'est à qui de jouer?** Whose turn is it?
le coup move	**le jeu** game	**le pari** bet			**C'est à toi de jouer.** It's your move.

les arts et loisirs créatifs • arts and crafts (1)

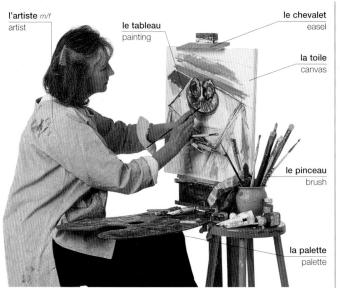

l'artiste *m/f*
artist

le tableau
painting

le chevalet
easel

la toile
canvas

le pinceau
brush

la palette
palette

la peinture | painting

les couleurs • colors

rouge
red

bleu
blue

jaune
yellow

vert
green

orange
orange

violet
purple

blanc
white

noir
black

gris
gray

rose
pink

marron
brown

indigo
indigo

les couleurs
paints

la peinture à l'huile
oil paint

l'aquarelle
watercolor paint

les pastels
pastels

l'acrylique
acrylic paint

la gouache
poster paint

les autres arts • other crafts

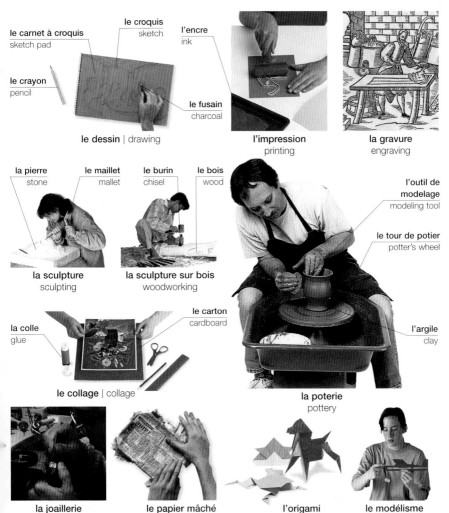

le carnet à croquis
sketch pad

le croquis
sketch

l'encre
ink

le crayon
pencil

le fusain
charcoal

le dessin | drawing

l'impression
printing

la gravure
engraving

la pierre
stone

le maillet
mallet

le burin
chisel

le bois
wood

l'outil de modelage
modeling tool

le tour de potier
potter's wheel

la sculpture
sculpting

la sculpture sur bois
woodworking

la colle
glue

le carton
cardboard

l'argile
clay

le collage | collage

la poterie
pottery

la joaillerie
jewelry-making

le papier mâché
papier-mâché

l'origami
origami

le modélisme
model-making

les arts et loisirs créatifs • arts and crafts (2)

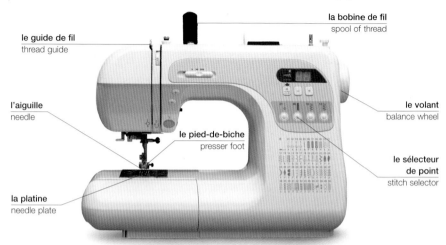

la bobine de fil
spool of thread

le guide de fil
thread guide

l'aiguille
needle

le pied-de-biche
presser foot

le volant
balance wheel

le sélecteur
de point
stitch selector

la platine
needle plate

la machine à coudre | sewing machine

les ciseaux
scissors

le patron
pattern

la pelote à épingles
pincushion

l'épingle
pin

le mètre ruban
tape measure

le tissu
material

la corbeille à couture | sewing basket

le fil
thread

l'œillet
eye

la bobine
bobbin

l'agrafe
hook

le dé à coudre
thimble

la craie de tailleur
tailor's chalk

le mannequin
tailor's form

le point | stitch

enfiler
thread (v)

coudre
sew (v)

repriser
darn (v)

faufiler
tack (v)

couper
cut (v)

la tapisserie
needlepoint

la broderie
embroidery

le crochet | crochet hook

le crochet
crochet

le macramé
macramé

le patchwork
patchwork

le fuseau | lace bobbin

le métier à tisser | loom

le quilting
quilting

la dentelle
lacemaking

le tissage
weaving

vocabulaire • vocabulary

défaire unpick (v)	**le nylon** nylon
le tissu fabric	**la soie** silk
le coton cotton	**la fermeture éclair** zipper
le lin linen	**la mode** fashion
le polyester polyester	**le styliste** *m* **la styliste** *f* designer

l'aiguille à tricoter | knitting needle

la laine | yarn

le tricot | knitting

l'écheveau | skein

l'environnement
environment

l'espace • space

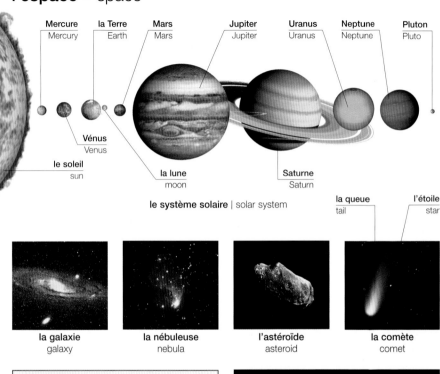

Mercure Mercury	**la Terre** Earth	**Mars** Mars	**Jupiter** Jupiter	**Uranus** Uranus	**Neptune** Neptune	**Pluton** Pluto

Vénus Venus

le soleil sun

la lune moon

Saturne Saturn

le système solaire | solar system

la queue tail

l'étoile star

la galaxie galaxy	**la nébuleuse** nebula	**l'astéroïde** asteroid	**la comète** comet

vocabulaire • vocabulary

l'univers universe	**le trou noir** black hole	**la pleine lune** full moon
l'orbite orbit	**la planète** planet	**la nouvelle lune** new moon
la pesanteur gravity	**le météore** meteor	**le croissant de lune** crescent moon

l'éclipse | eclipse

l'exploration spatiale • space exploration

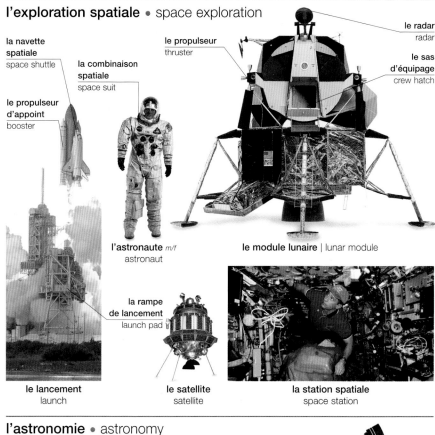

la navette spatiale
space shuttle

le propulseur
thruster

le radar
radar

la combinaison spatiale
space suit

le sas d'équipage
crew hatch

le propulseur d'appoint
booster

l'astronaute *m/f*
astronaut

le module lunaire | lunar module

la rampe de lancement
launch pad

le lancement
launch

le satellite
satellite

la station spatiale
space station

l'astronomie • astronomy

la constellation
constellation

les jumelles
binoculars

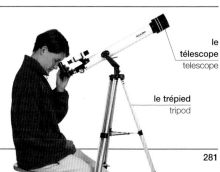

le télescope
telescope

le trépied
tripod

la terre • Earth

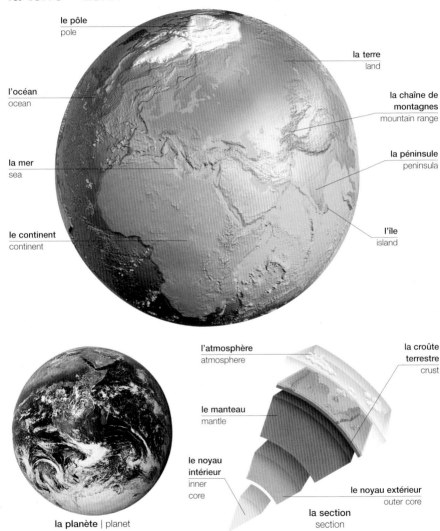

le pôle
pole

la terre
land

l'océan
ocean

la chaîne de
montagnes
mountain range

la péninsule
peninsula

la mer
sea

le continent
continent

l'île
island

l'atmosphère
atmosphere

la croûte
terrestre
crust

le manteau
mantle

le noyau
intérieur
inner
core

le noyau extérieur
outer core

la planète | planet

la section
section

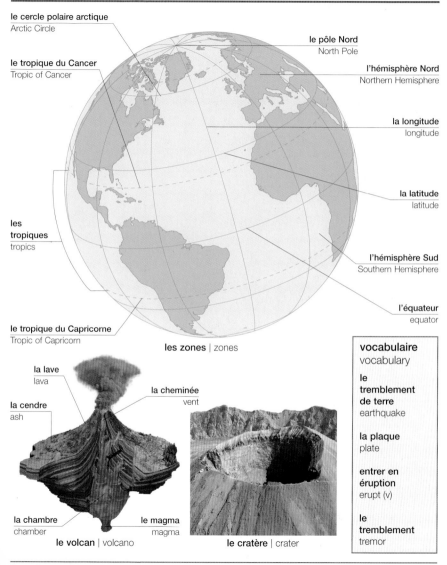

le cercle polaire arctique
Arctic Circle

le tropique du Cancer
Tropic of Cancer

le pôle Nord
North Pole

l'hémisphère Nord
Northern Hemisphere

la longitude
longitude

la latitude
latitude

les tropiques
tropics

l'hémisphère Sud
Southern Hemisphere

l'équateur
equator

le tropique du Capricorne
Tropic of Capricorn

les zones | zones

la lave
lava

la cheminée
vent

la cendre
ash

la chambre
chamber

le magma
magma

le volcan | volcano

le cratère | crater

vocabulaire
vocabulary

le tremblement de terre
earthquake

la plaque
plate

entrer en éruption
erupt (v)

le tremblement
tremor

le paysage • landscape

la montagne
mountain

la pente
slope

la rive
bank

la rivière
river

les rapides
rapids

les rochers
rocks

le glacier
glacier

la vallée | valley

la colline
hill

le plateau
plateau

la gorge
gorge

la caverne
cave

la plaine | plain

le désert | desert

la forêt | forest

le bois | woods

la forêt tropicale
rain forest

le marais
swamp

le pré
meadow

la prairie
grassland

la cascade
waterfall

le ruisseau
stream

le lac
lake

le geyser
geyser

la côte
coast

la falaise
cliff

le récif de corail
coral reef

l'estuaire
estuary

le temps • weather

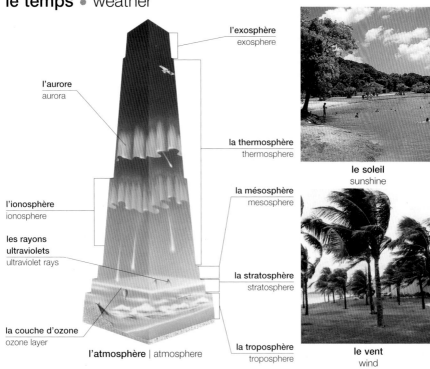

l'exosphère
exosphere

l'aurore
aurora

la thermosphère
thermosphere

le soleil
sunshine

la mésosphère
mesosphere

l'ionosphère
ionosphere

les rayons
ultraviolets
ultraviolet rays

la stratosphère
stratosphere

la couche d'ozone
ozone layer

l'atmosphère | atmosphere

la troposphère
troposphere

le vent
wind

---

vocabulaire • vocabulary

la neige fondue sleet	l'averse shower	(très) chaud hot	sec dry	venteux windy	J'ai chaud / froid. I'm hot / cold.
la grêle hail	ensoleillé sunny	froid cold	mouillé wet	la tempête gale	Il pleut. It's raining.
le tonnerre thunder	nuageux cloudy	chaud warm	moite humid	la température temperature	Il fait… degrés. It's… degrees.

l'éclair
lightning

le nuage
cloud

la pluie
rain

l'orage
storm

la brume
mist

le brouillard
fog

l'arc-en-ciel
rainbow

le glaçon
icicle

la neige
snow

le givre
frost

la glace
ice

le gel
freeze

l'ouragan
hurricane

la tornade
tornado

la mousson
monsoon

l'inondation
flood

les roches • rocks

igné • igneous

le granit
granite

l'obsidienne
obsidian

le basalte
basalt

la pierre ponce
pumice

sédimentaire • sedimentary

le grès
sandstone

le calcaire
limestone

la craie
chalk

le silex
flint

le conglomérat
conglomerate

le charbon
coal

métamorphique
metamorphic

l'ardoise
slate

le schiste
schist

le gneiss
gneiss

le marbre
marble

les gemmes • gems

le rubis
ruby

l'aigue-marine
aquamarine

l'améthyste
amethyst

le diamant
diamond

le jade
jade

le jais
jet

l'émeraude
emerald

l'opale
opal

le saphir
sapphire

la pierre de lune
moonstone

le grenat
garnet

le topaze
topaz

la tourmaline
tourmaline

les minéraux • minerals

le quartz
quartz

le mica
mica

le soufre
sulfur

l'hématite
hematite

la calcite
calcite

la malachite
malachite

la turquoise
turquoise

l'onyx
onyx

l'agate
agate

le graphite
graphite

les métaux • metals

l'or
gold

l'argent
silver

le platine
platinum

le nickel
nickel

le fer
iron

le cuivre
copper

l'étain
tin

l'aluminium
aluminum

le mercure
mercury

le zinc
zinc

les animaux • animals (1)

les mammifères • mammals

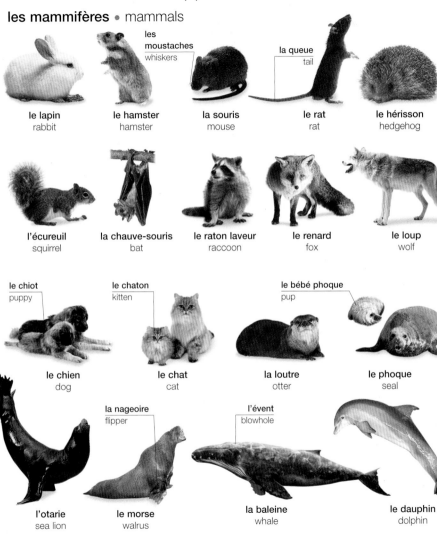

le lapin
rabbit

le hamster
hamster

les **moustaches**
whiskers

la souris
mouse

la queue
tail

le rat
rat

le hérisson
hedgehog

l'écureuil
squirrel

la chauve-souris
bat

le raton laveur
raccoon

le renard
fox

le loup
wolf

le chiot
puppy

le chaton
kitten

le bébé phoque
pup

le chien
dog

le chat
cat

la loutre
otter

le phoque
seal

la nageoire
flipper

l'évent
blowhole

l'otarie
sea lion

le morse
walrus

la baleine
whale

le dauphin
dolphin

la ramure
antler

la crinière
mane

la bosse
hump

le sabot
hoof

le cerf
deer

le zèbre
zebra

la girafe
giraffe

le chameau
camel

la trompe
trunk

la défense
tusk

la corne
horn

l'hippopotame
hippopotamus

l'éléphant
elephant

le rhinocéros
rhinoceros

le tigre
tiger

la crinière
mane

le lion
lion

le singe
monkey

le gorille
gorilla

le koala
koala

la poche
pouch

le panda
panda

la griffe
claw

le kangourou
kangaroo

l'ours
bear

l'ours blanc
polar bear

français • english

les animaux • animals (2)

les oiseaux • birds

le canari
canary

le moineau
sparrow

le colibri
hummingbird

la queue
tail

l'hirondelle
swallow

le corbeau
crow

le pigeon
pigeon

le pic
woodpecker

le faucon
falcon

la chouette
owl

le goéland
gull

l'aigle
eagle

le pélican
pelican

le flamant rose
flamingo

la cigogne
stork

la grue
crane

le pingouin
penguin

l'autruche
ostrich

les reptiles • reptiles

l'oie | goose

le cygne
swan

le paon
peacock

le faisan
pheasant

le dindon
turkey

le bec
beak

la plume
feather

l'aile
wing

le cacatoès
cockatoo

la griffe
claw

le perroquet
parrot

les écailles
scales

l'alligator
alligator

le lézard
lizard

l'iguane
iguana

la carapace
shell

la tortue marine
turtle

la tortue
tortoise

le serpent
snake

le museau
snout

le crocodile
crocodile

les animaux • animals (3)

les amphibiens • amphibians

la grenouille
frog

le crapaud
toad

le têtard
tadpole

la salamandre
salamander

les poissons • fish

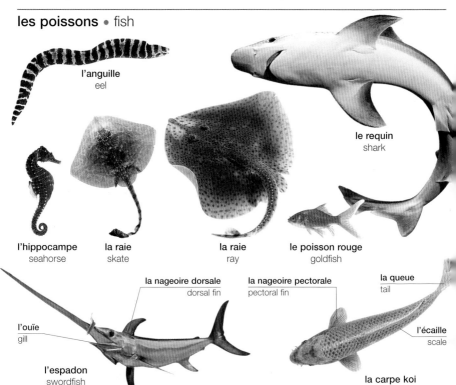

l'anguille
eel

le requin
shark

l'hippocampe
seahorse

la raie
skate

la raie
ray

le poisson rouge
goldfish

la nageoire dorsale
dorsal fin

la nageoire pectorale
pectoral fin

la queue
tail

l'ouïe
gill

l'écaille
scale

l'espadon
swordfish

la carpe koi
koi

les invertébrés • invertebrates

la fourmi
ant

le termite
termite

l'abeille
bee

la guêpe
wasp

le scarabée
beetle

le cafard
cockroach

le papillon de nuit
moth

l'antenne
antenna
le papillon
butterfly

le cocon
cocoon

la chenille
caterpillar

le cricket
cricket

la sauterelle
grasshopper

la mante religieuse
praying mantis

le dard
sting
le scorpion
scorpion

le mille-pattes
centipede

la libellule
dragonfly

la mouche
fly

le moustique
mosquito

la coccinelle
ladybug

l'araignée
spider

la limace
slug

l'escargot
snail

le ver
worm

l'étoile de mer
starfish

la moule
mussel

le crabe
crab

le homard
lobster

la pieuvre
octopus

le calmar
squid

la méduse
jellyfish

les plantes • plants

l'arbre • tree

la branche
branch

la feuille
leaf

la brindille
twig

le saule
willow

l'écorce
bark

le tronc
trunk

la racine
root

le chêne
oak

le peuplier
poplar

l'eucalyptus
eucalyptus

le mélèze
larch

le hêtre
beech

le bouleau
birch

le pin
pine

le cèdre
cedar

l'érable
maple

l'orme
elm

le tilleul
lime

la baie
berry

le houx
holly

le palmier
palm

la plante à fleurs • flowering plant

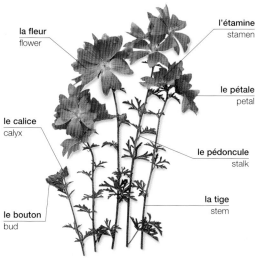

la fleur
flower

l'étamine
stamen

le pétale
petal

le calice
calyx

le pédoncule
stalk

la tige
stem

le bouton
bud

la renoncule
buttercup

la pâquerette
daisy

le chardon
thistle

le pissenlit
dandelion

la bruyère
heather

le coquelicot
poppy

la digitale
foxglove

le chèvrefeuille
honeysuckle

le tournesol
sunflower

le trèfle
clover

les jacinthes
des bois
bluebells

la primevère
primrose

les lupins
lupines

l'ortie
nettle

la ville • city

la ruelle
alley

l'immeuble
apartment block

la rue
street

la borne
barrier

la place
square

le magasin
store

le coin de la rue
street corner

le bord du
trottoir
curb

le trottoir
sidewalk

le parking
parking lot

la voie à
sens unique
one-way system

le lampadaire
streetlight

les bâtiments • buildings

la mairie
town hall

la bibliothèque
library

le cinéma
movie theater

le théâtre
theater

l'université
university

le gratte-ciel
skyscraper

la zone industrielle
industrial park

le centre-ville
downtown

la banlieue
suburb

le village
village

les environs • areas

l'école
school

---

vocabulaire • vocabulary

la zone piétonne pedestrian zone	**l'immeuble de bureaux** office block	**la place** square	**l'arrêt de bus** bus stop	**l'usine** factory
l'avenue avenue	**la rue transversale** side street	**la bouche d'égout** manhole	**le caniveau** gutter	**l'église** church

l'architecture • architecture

les bâtiments et structures • buildings and structures

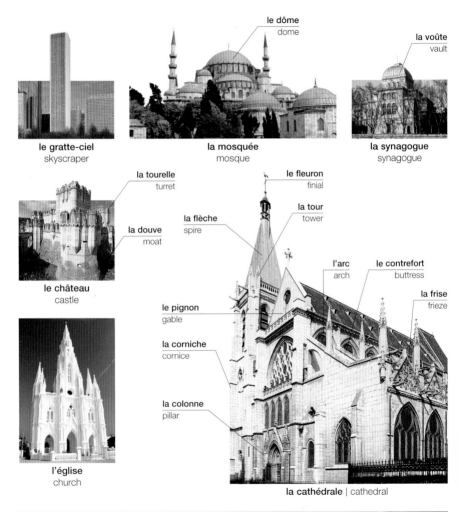

le dôme
dome

la voûte
vault

le gratte-ciel
skyscraper

la mosquée
mosque

la synagogue
synagogue

la tourelle
turret

le fleuron
finial

la tour
tower

la flèche
spire

la douve
moat

l'arc
arch

le contrefort
buttress

le château
castle

la frise
frieze

le pignon
gable

la corniche
cornice

la colonne
pillar

l'église
church

la cathédrale | cathedral

le barrage
dam

le pont
bridge

le temple
temple

les styles • styles

l'architrave
architrave

le chœur
choir

gothique
Gothic

Renaissance
Renaissance

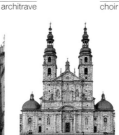

baroque
Baroque

rococo
Rococo

le fronton
pediment

néoclassique
Neoclassical

art nouveau
Art Nouveau

art déco
Art Deco

l'information
reference

l'heure • time

la grande aiguille
minute hand

la petite aiguille
hour hand

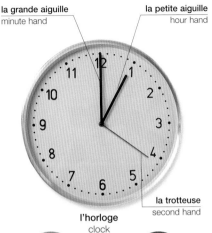

l'horloge
clock

la trotteuse
second hand

vocabulaire • vocabulary

la seconde second	**maintenant** now	**un quart** **d'heure** a quarter of an hour
la minute minute	**plus tard** later	
		vingt minutes twenty minutes
l'heure hour	**une demi-** **heure** half an hour	
		quarante **minutes** forty minutes

Quelle heure est-il?
What time is it?

Il est trois heures.
It's three o'clock.

une heure cinq
five past one

une heure dix
ten past one

une heure et quart
quarter past one

une heure vingt
twenty past one

une heure vingt-cinq
twenty-five past one

une heure trente
one thirty

deux heures moins
vingt-cinq
twenty-five to two

deux heures moins
vingt
twenty to two

deux heures moins
le quart
quarter to two

deux heures moins dix
ten to two

deux heures
moins cinq
five to two

deux heures
two o'clock

la nuit et le jour • night and day

minuit
midnight

le lever du soleil
sunrise

l'aube
dawn

le matin
morning

le coucher du soleil
sunset

le midi
noon

le crépuscule
dusk

le soir
evening

l'après-midi
afternoon

vocabulaire • vocabulary

tôt
early

à l'heure
on time

tard
late

Tu es en avance.
You're early.

Tu es en retard.
You're late.

J'arrive bientôt.
I'll be there soon.

Sois à l'heure, s'il te plaît.
Please be on time.

À tout à l'heure.
I'll see you later.

Ça commence à quelle heure?
What time does it start?

Ça finit à quelle heure?
What time does it end?

Il se fait tard.
It's getting late.

Ça dure combien de temps?
How long will it last?

le calendrier • calendar

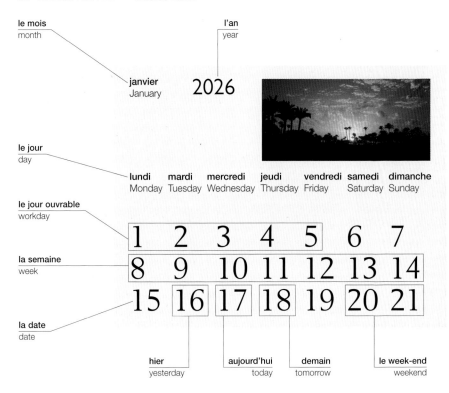

le mois
month

l'an
year

janvier
January

2026

le jour
day

lundi	mardi	mercredi	jeudi	vendredi	samedi	dimanche
Monday	Tuesday	Wednesday	Thursday	Friday	Saturday	Sunday

le jour ouvrable
workday

la semaine
week

1	2	3	4	5	6	7
8	9	10	11	12	13	14
15	16	17	18	19	20	21

la date
date

hier
yesterday

aujourd'hui
today

demain
tomorrow

le week-end
weekend

vocabulaire • vocabulary

janvier	mars	mai	juillet	septembre	novembre
January	March	May	July	September	November
février	avril	juin	août	octobre	décembre
February	April	June	August	October	December

les ans • years

1900 mille neuf cents • nineteen hundred

1901 mille neuf cent un • nineteen oh one

1910 mille neuf cent dix • nineteen ten

2000 deux mille • two thousand

2001 deux mille un • two thousand and one

les saisons • seasons

le printemps
spring

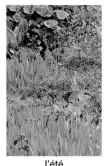
l'été
summer

l'automne
fall

l'hiver
winter

vocabulaire • vocabulary

le siècle
century

la décennie
decade

le millénaire
millennium

quinze jours
two weeks

cette semaine
this week

la semaine dernière
last week

la semaine prochaine
next week

avant-hier
the day before yesterday

après-demain
the day after tomorrow

hebdomadaire
weekly

mensuel
monthly

annuel
annual

Quelle est la date aujourd'hui?
What's the date today?

C'est le sept février.
It's February the seventh.

les nombres • numbers

0	**zéro** • zero		20	**vingt** • twenty
1	**un** • one		21	**vingt et un** • twenty-one
2	**deux** • two		22	**vingt-deux** • twenty-two
3	**trois** • three		30	**trente** • thirty
4	**quatre** • four		40	**quarante** • forty
5	**cinq** • five		50	**cinquante** • fifty
6	**six** • six		60	**soixante** • sixty
7	**sept** • seven		70	**soixante-dix** • seventy
8	**huit** • eight		80	**quatre-vingts** • eighty
9	**neuf** • nine		90	**quatre-vingt-dix** • ninety
10	**dix** • ten		100	**cent** • one hundred
11	**onze** • eleven		110	**cent dix** • one hundred ten
12	**douze** • twelve		200	**deux cents** • two hundred
13	**treize** • thirteen		300	**trois cents** • three hundred
14	**quatorze** • fourteen		400	**quatre cents** • four hundred
15	**quinze** • fifteen		500	**cinq cents** • five hundred
16	**seize** • sixteen		600	**six cents** • six hundred
17	**dix-sept** • seventeen		700	**sept cents** • seven hundred
18	**dix-huit** • eighteen		800	**huit cents** • eight hundred
19	**dix-neuf** • nineteen		900	**neuf cents** • nine hundred

1,000   **mille** • one thousand

10,000   **dix mille** • ten thousand

20,000   **vingt mille** • twenty thousand

50,000   **cinquante mille** • fifty thousand

55,500   **cinqante-cinq mille cinq cents** • fifty-five thousand five hundred

100,000   **cent mille** • one hundred thousand

1,000,000   **un million** • one million

1,000,000,000   **un milliard** • one billion

premier *m*
première *f*
first

deuxième
second

troisième
third

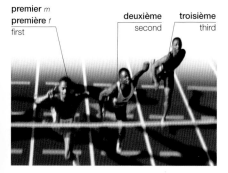

quatrième • fourth

cinquième • fifth

sixième • sixth

septième • seventh

huitième • eighth

neuvième • ninth

dixième • tenth

onzième • eleventh

douzième • twelfth

treizième • thirteenth

quatorzième • fourteenth

quinzième • fifteenth

seizième
sixteenth

dix-septième
seventeenth

dix-huitième
eighteenth

dix-neuvième
nineteenth

vingtième
twentieth

vingt et unième
twenty-first

vingt-deuxième
twenty-second

vingt-troisième
twenty-third

trentième
thirtieth

quarantième
fortieth

cinquantième
fiftieth

soixantième
sixtieth

soixante-dixième
seventieth

quatre-vingtième
eightieth

quatre-vingt-dixième
ninetieth

centième
(one) hundredth

les poids et mesures • weights and measures

la superficie • area

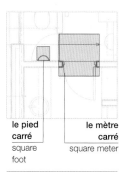

le pied carré
square foot

le mètre carré
square meter

la distance
distance

le kilomètre
kilometer

le mile
mile

le plateau
pan

la livre
pound

le kilogramme
kilogram

l'once
ounce

KRUPS

le gramme
gram

la balance | scale

vocabulaire • vocabulary

le yard yard	**la tonne** ton	**mesurer** measure (v)
le mètre meter	**le milligramme** milligram	**peser** weigh (v)

la longueur • length

le pied
foot

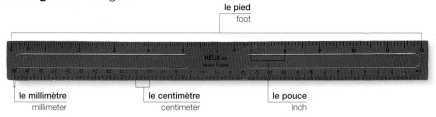

HELIX 835
Made in England

le millimètre
millimeter

le centimètre
centimeter

le pouce
inch

la capacité • capacity

le demi-litre
half-liter

la pinte
pint

le volume
volume

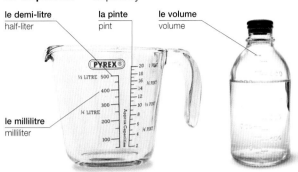

le millilitre
milliliter

le verre mesureur
measuring cup

la mesure pour les liquides
liquid measure

le récipient • container

la brique
carton

le paquet
packet

la bouteille
bottle

le sac
bag

la barquette | tub

le pot | jar

la boîte | tin

le pulvérisateur
spray bottle

le pain
bar

le tube
tube

le rouleau
roll

la canette
can

la bombe aérosol
spray can

la carte du monde • world map

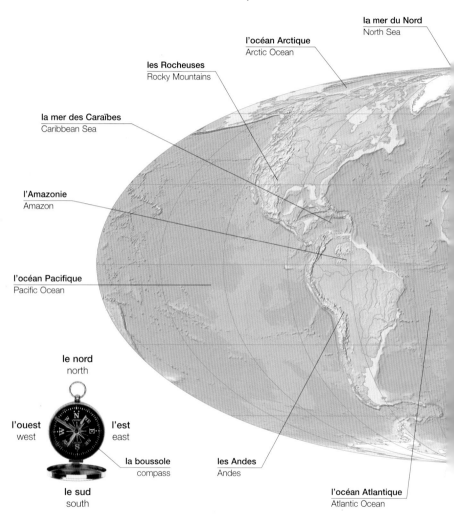

la mer du Nord
North Sea

l'océan Arctique
Arctic Ocean

les Rocheuses
Rocky Mountains

la mer des Caraïbes
Caribbean Sea

l'Amazonie
Amazon

l'océan Pacifique
Pacific Ocean

le nord
north

l'ouest
west

l'est
east

la boussole
compass

les Andes
Andes

l'océan Atlantique
Atlantic Ocean

le sud
south

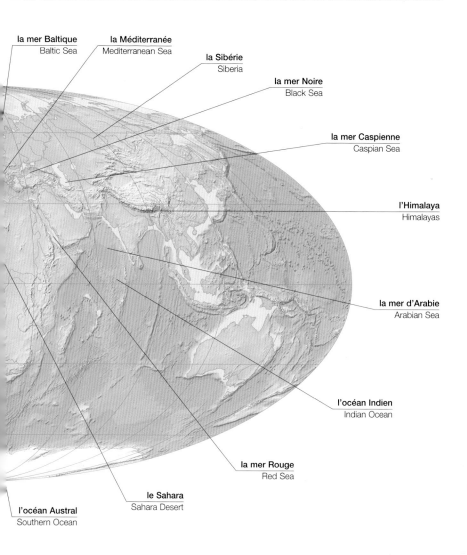

la mer Baltique
Baltic Sea

la Méditerranée
Mediterranean Sea

la Sibérie
Siberia

la mer Noire
Black Sea

la mer Caspienne
Caspian Sea

l'Himalaya
Himalayas

la mer d'Arabie
Arabian Sea

l'océan Indien
Indian Ocean

la mer Rouge
Red Sea

le Sahara
Sahara Desert

l'océan Austral
Southern Ocean

l'Amérique du Nord et centrale
North and Central America

la Barbade • Barbados

le Canada • Canada

le Costa Rica • Costa Rica

Cuba • Cuba

la Jamaïque • Jamaica

le Mexique • Mexico

le Panama • Panama

Trinité-et-Tobago • Trinidad and Tobago

les États-Unis d'Amérique
United States of America

Antigua-et-Barbuda
Antigua and Barbuda

les Bahamas • Bahamas

la Barbade • Barbados

le Bélize • Belize

le Canada • Canada

le Costa Rica • Costa Rica

Cuba • Cuba

la Dominique • Dominica

les États-Unis d'Amérique
United States of America

la Grenade • Grenada

le Groenland • Greenland

le Guatemala • Guatemala

Haïti • Haiti

Hawaï • Hawaii

le Honduras • Honduras

la Jamaïque • Jamaica

le Mexique • Mexico

le Nicaragua • Nicaragua

le Panama • Panama

Porto Rico • Puerto Rico

la République dominicaine
Dominican Republic

Saint-Kitts-et-Nevis
St. Kitts and Nevis

Saint-Vincent-et-les-Grenadines • St. Vincent and the Grenadines

Sainte-Lucie • St. Lucia

le Salvador • El Salvador

Trinité-et-Tobago
Trinidad and Tobago

l'Amérique du Sud • South America

l'**Argentine** • Argentina

la **Bolivie** • Bolivia

le **Brésil** • Brazil

le **Chili** • Chile

la **Colombie** • Colombia

l'**Équateur** • Ecuador

le **Pérou** • Peru

l'**Uruguay** • Uruguay

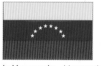

le **Venezuela** • Venezuela

l'**Argentine** • Argentina
la **Bolivie** • Bolivia
le **Brésil** • Brazil
le **Chili** • Chile
la **Colombie** • Colombia
l'**Équateur** • Ecuador
le **Guyana** • Guyana
la **Guyane française**
French Guiana
les **îles Galapagos**
Galápagos Islands
les **îles Malouines**
Falkland Islands
le **Paraguay** • Paraguay

le **Pérou** • Peru
le **Surinam** • Suriname
l'**Uruguay** • Uruguay
le **Venezuela** • Venezuela

vocabulaire • vocabulary	
le pays country	**la colonie** colony
la nation nation	**la principauté** principality
l'État state	**la zone** zone
le continent continent	**le district** district
la province province	**la région** region
le territoire territory	**la capitale** capital

l'Europe • Europe

la France • France

l'Allemagne • Germany

l'Italie • Italy

la Pologne • Poland

le Portugal • Portugal

l'Espagne • Spain

l'Albanie • Albania
l'Allemagne • Germany
l'Andorre • Andorra
l'Angleterre • England
l'Autriche • Austria
les Baléares • Balearic Islands
le Bélarus • Belarus
la Belgique • Belgium
la Bosnie-Herzégovine
Bosnia and Herzegovina
la Bulgarie • Bulgaria
Chypre • Cyprus
la Corse • Corsica
la Croatie • Croatia
le Danemark • Denmark
l'Écosse • Scotland
l'Espagne • Spain
l'Estonie • Estonia
la Fédération de Russie
Russian Federation
la Finlande • Finland
la France • France

la Grèce • Greece
la Hongrie • Hungary
l'Irlande • Ireland
l'Irlande du Nord
Northern Ireland
l'Islande • Iceland
l'Italie • Italy
Kaliningrad • Kaliningrad
le Kosovo • Kosovo
la Lettonie • Latvia
le Liechtenstein • Liechtenstein
la Lituanie • Lithuania
le Luxembourg • Luxembourg
la Macédonie du Nord
North Macedonia
Malte • Malta
la Moldavie • Moldova
Monaco • Monaco
le Monténégro • Montenegro
la Norvège • Norway
les Pays-Bas • Netherlands
les Pays de Galles • Wales

la Pologne • Poland
le Portugal • Portugal
la République tchèque
Czech Republic
la Roumanie • Romania
le Royaume-Uni
United Kingdom
Saint-Marin • San Marino
la Sardaigne • Sardinia
la Serbie • Serbia
la Sicile • Sicily
la Slovaquie • Slovakia
la Slovénie • Slovenia
la Suède • Sweden
la Suisse • Switzerland
l'Ukraine • Ukraine
le Vatican • Vatican City

l'Afrique • Africa

l'**Égypte** • Egypt

l'**Éthiopie** • Ethiopia

le **Kenya** • Kenya

le **Nigéria** • Nigeria

l'**Afrique du Sud** • South Africa

l'**Ouganda** • Uganda

l'**Afrique du Sud** • South Africa

l'**Algérie** • Algeria

l'**Angola** • Angola

le **Bénin** • Benin

le **Botswana** • Botswana

le **Burkina Faso** • Burkina Faso

le **Burundi** • Burundi

le **Cameroun** • Cameroon

les **Comores** • Comoros

le **Congo** • Congo

la **Côte d'Ivoire** • Ivory Coast

Djibouti • Djibouti

l'**Égypte** • Egypt

l'**Érythrée** • Eritrea

l'**Eswatini** • Eswatini

l'**Éthiopie** • Ethiopia

le **Gabon** • Gabon

la **Gambie** • Gambia

le **Ghana** • Ghana

la **Guinée** • Guinea

la **Guinée-Bissau**
Guinea-Bissau

la **Guinée équatoriale**
Equatorial Guinea

Maurice • Mauritius

le **Kenya** • Kenya

le **Lesotho** • Lesotho

le **Libéria** • Liberia

la **Libye** • Libya

Madagascar • Madagascar

le **Malawi** • Malawi

le **Mali** • Mali

le **Maroc** • Morocco

la **Mauritanie** • Mauritania

le **Mozambique** • Mozambique

la **Namibie** • Namibia

le **Niger** • Niger

le **Nigéria** • Nigeria

l'**Ouganda** • Uganda

la **République centrafricaine**
Central African Republic

la **République démocratique
du Congo** • Democratic Republic
of the Congo

le **Rwanda** • Rwanda

le **Sahara occidental**
Western Sahara

Sao Tomé-et-Principe
São Tomé and Príncipe

le **Sénégal** • Senegal

la **Sierra Leone** • Sierra Leone

la **Somalie** • Somalia

le **Soudan** • Sudan

le **Soudan du Sud** • South Sudan

la **Tanzanie** • Tanzania

le **Tchad** • Chad

le **Togo** • Togo

la **Tunisie** • Tunisia

la **Zambie** • Zambia

le **Zimbabwe** • Zimbabwe

l'Asie • Asia

le Bangladesh • Bangladesh

la Chine • China

l'Inde • India

le Japon • Japan

la Jordanie • Jordan

les Philippines • Philippines

la Corée du Sud • South Korea

la Thaïlande • Thailand

la Turquie • Türkiye (Turkey)

l'Afghanistan • Afghanistan
l'Arabie saoudite • Saudi Arabia
l'Arménie • Armenia
l'Azerbaïdjan • Azerbaijan
Bahreïn • Bahrain
le Bangladesh • Bangladesh
le Bhoutan • Bhutan
le Brunei • Brunei
le Cambodge • Cambodia
la Chine • China
la Corée du Nord • North Korea
la Corée du Sud • South Korea
les Émirats arabes unis
United Arab Emirates
la Géorgie • Georgia

l'Inde • India
l'Indonésie • Indonesia
l'Irak • Iraq
l'Iran • Iran
Israël • Israel
le Japon • Japan
la Jordanie • Jordan
le Kazakhstan • Kazakhstan
le Kirghizistan • Kyrgyzstan
le Koweït • Kuwait
le Laos • Laos
le Liban • Lebanon
la Malaisie • Malaysia
les Maldives • Maldives

la Mongolie • Mongolia
le Myanmar (la Birmanie)
Myanmar (Burma)
le Népal • Nepal
l'Oman • Oman
l'Ouzbékistan • Uzbekistan
le Pakistan • Pakistan
les Philippines • Philippines
le Qatar • Qatar
Singapour • Singapore
le Sri Lanka • Sri Lanka
la Syrie • Syria
le Tadjikistan • Tajikistan
la Thaïlande • Thailand

l'Indonésie • Indonesia

l'Arabie saoudite • Saudi Arabia

le Vietnam • Vietnam

le Timor oriental • East Timor
le Turkménistan • Turkmenistan
la Turquie • Türkiye (Turkey)
le Vietnam • Vietnam
le Yémen • Yemen

l'Oceanía
Oceania

l'Australie • Australia

la Nouvelle-Zélande • New Zealand

l'Australie • Australia
Fidji • Fiji
les îles Salomon • Solomon Islands
la Nouvelle-Zélande • New Zealand
la Papouasie-Nouvelle-Guinée Papua New Guinea
la Tasmanie • Tasmania
Vanuatu • Vanuatu

particules et antonymes • particles and antonyms

à to	**de** from	**pour** for	**vers** toward
au-dessus de over	**sous** under	**le long de** along	**à travers** across
devant in front of	**derrière** behind	**avec** with	**sans** without
sur onto	**dans** into	**avant** before	**après** after
dans in	**dehors** out	**avant** by	**jusqu'à** until
au-dessus de above	**au-dessous de** below	**tôt** early	**tard** late
à l'intérieur de inside	**à l'extérieur de** outside	**maintenant** now	**plus tard** later
en haut up	**en bas** down	**toujours** always	**jamais** never
à at	**au-delà de** beyond	**souvent** often	**rarement** rarely
à travers through	**autour de** around	**hier** yesterday	**demain** tomorrow
sur on top of	**à côté de** beside	**premier** m **première** f first	**dernier** m **dernière** f last
entre between	**en face de** opposite	**chaque** every	**quelque** some
près de near	**loin de** far	**vers** about	**exactement** exactly
ici here	**là** there	**un peu** a little	**beaucoup** a lot

grand m / **grande** f
large

petit m / **petite** f
small

bruyant m
bruyante f
noisy

silencieux m
silencieuse f
quiet

large
wide

étroit m / **étroite** f
narrow

chaud m / **chaude** f
hot

froid m / **froide** f
cold

grand m / **grande** f
tall

petit m / **petite** f
short

ouvert m / **ouverte** f
open

fermé m / **fermée** f
closed

haut m / **haute** f
high

bas m / **basse** f
low

plein m / **pleine** f
full

vide
empty

épais m / **épaisse** f
thick

fin m / **fine** f
thin

neuf m / **neuve** f
new

vieux m / **vieille** f
old

léger m / **légère** f
light

lourd m / **lourde** f
heavy

éclairé m / **éclairée** f
light

sombre
dark

dur m / **dure** f
hard

mou m / **molle** f
soft

facile
easy

difficile
difficult

humide
wet

sec m / **sèche** f
dry

libre
free

occupé m / **occupée** f
occupied

bon m / **bonne** f
good

mauvais m / **mauvaise** f
bad

fort m / **forte** f
strong

faible
weak

rapide
fast

lent m / **lente** f
slow

gros m / **grosse** f
fat

mince
thin

correct m / **correcte** f
correct

faux m / **fausse** f
wrong

jeune
young

vieux m / **vieille** f
old

propre
clean

sale
dirty

mieux
better

pire
worse

beau m / **belle** f
beautiful

laid m / **laide** f
ugly

noir m / **noire** f
black

blanc m / **blanche** f
white

cher m / **chère** f
expensive

bon marché
cheap

intéressant m
intéressante f
interesting

ennuyeux m
ennuyeuse f
boring

malade
sick

bien
well

le début
beginning

la fin
end

phrases utiles • useful phrases

**phrases
essentielles**
essential
phrases

Oui
Yes

Non
No

Peut-être
Maybe

S'il vous plaît
Please

Merci
Thank you

De rien
You're welcome

Pardon
Excuse me

Je suis désolé *m*
Je suis désolée *f*
I'm sorry

Ne… pas
Don't

D'accord
OK

Très bien
That's fine

C'est juste
That's correct

C'est faux
That's wrong

salutations
greetings

Bonjour
Hello

Au revoir
Goodbye

Bonjour
Good morning

Bonjour
Good afternoon

Bonsoir
Good evening

Bonne nuit
Good night

Comment allez-vous?
How are you?

Je m'appelle…
My name is…

**Vous vous appelez
comment?**
What is your name?

**Il / Elle s'appelle
comment?**
What is his / her name?

Je vous présente…
May I introduce…

C'est…
This is…

Enchanté *m*
Enchantée *f*
Pleased to meet you

À tout à l'heure
See you later

panneaux • signs

Office de tourisme
Tourist information

Entrée
Entrance

Sortie
Exit

Sortie de secours
Emergency exit

Poussez
Push

Danger
Danger

Défense de fumer
No smoking

En panne
Out of order

Heures d'ouverture
Opening times

Entrée gratuite
Free admission

Réduit
Reduced

Soldes
Sale

**l'accès pour
fauteuil roulant**
Wheelchair access

assistance
help

Je suis sourd *m*
Je suis sourde *f*
I am deaf

Je suis aveugle
I am blind

**Pouvez-vous
m'aider?**
Can you help me?

Je ne comprends pas
I don't understand

Je ne sais pas
I don't know

Parlez-vous anglais?
Do you speak
English?

Je parle anglais
I speak English

**Parlez moins vite,
s'il vous plaît**
Please speak
more slowly

**Écrivez-le pour moi,
s'il vous plaît**
Please write it down
for me

J'ai perdu…
I have lost…

directions
directions

Je me suis perdu
I am lost

Où est le / la… ?
Where is the… ?

**Où est le / la…
le / la plus proche?**
Where is the nearest… ?

Où sont les toilettes?
Where is the restroom?

Pour aller à… ?
How do I get to… ?

À droite
To the right

À gauche
To the left

Tout droit
Straight ahead

C'est loin… ?
How far is… ?

les panneaux routiers
road signs

Prudence
Caution

Entrée interdite
Do not enter

Ralentir
Slow down

Déviation
Detour

Serrez à droite
Keep right

Autoroute
Freeway

Stationnement interdit
No parking

Impasse
Dead end

Cédez le passage
Yield

Sens unique
One-way street

Riverains autorisés
Residents only

Travaux
Roadwork

Virage dangereux
Dangerous curve

logement
accommodations

**J'ai réservé
une chambre**
I have a reservation

**Où est la salle
à manger?**
Where is the dining room?

**Le petit déjeuner est
à quelle heure?**
What time is breakfast?

**Je serai de retour
à… heures**
I'll be back at… o'clock

Je pars demain
I'm leaving tomorrow

nourriture et boissons
eating and drinking

À la vôtre!
Cheers!

**C'est délicieux /
terrible**
It's delicious / awful

Je ne bois / fume pas
I don't drink / smoke

**Je ne mange pas de
la viande**
I don't eat meat

**Je n'en veux plus,
merci**
No more for me, thank you

**Encore un peu,
s'il vous plaît**
May I have some more?

**L'addition, s'il
vous plaît**
May we have the check?

Je voudrais un reçu
Can I have a receipt?

Zone fumeur
smoking area

la santé
health

**Je ne me sens
pas bien**
I don't feel well

J'ai envie de vomir
I feel sick

**Va-t-il / va-t-elle
guérir?**
Will he / she be all right?

J'ai mal ici
It hurts here

J'ai de la fièvre
I have a fever

**Je suis enceinte
de… mois**
I'm… months pregnant

**J'ai besoin d'une
ordonnance pour…**
I need a prescription for…

**Je prends
habituellement…**
I normally take…

Je suis allergique à…
I'm allergic to…

Index français • French index

français

français

français

français

français

filtre à air m 202, 204
fin m / fine f 321
finance f 97
Finlande 316
fiole f 166
flageolets m 131
flamant rose m 292
flash m 270
flash compact m 270
flèche f 95, 249, 300
fléchettes f 273
fléchir 251
flétan m 120
fleur f 297
fleuret m 249
fleurette f 122
fleuriste m/f 188
fleuron m 300
fleurs f 110
fleurs séchées m 111
flexions de biceps f 251
florentin m 141
flotteur m 61, 244
flou 271
flûte f 139
flûte traversière f 257
fœtus m 52
foie m 18, 118
foin m 184
fois 165
follicule m 20
foncé 41
fond de robe m 35
fond de scène m 254
fond de teint m 40
fontaine m 85
football m 222
football américain m 220
forceps m 53, 167
forêt f 285
foret à béton m 80
foret à bois plat m 80
foret à métaux m 80
forets m 80
forets à bois m 80
forêt tropicale m 285
forme physique f 250
formes f 164
fort m / forte f 321
fosse d'orchestre f 254
fossette f 15
fou m 272
fouet m 68
fougère f 86
foulard m 36
four m 66
fourche m 88, 207
fourches f 39
fourchette f 65
fourchette à découper f 68
fourmi f 295
fournisseur d'accès m 177
fournitures de bureau 173
fourre-tout m 37
foyer m 255
fraction f 165

fracture f 46
fragile 98
frais m / fraîche f 121, 127, 130
frais bancaires m 96
fraise f 127
fraise m 50
framboise f 127
France 316
frapper 223, 224, 225
freesia m 110
freezer m 67
frein m 200, 204, 206
frein à main m 203
freiner 207
fréquence f 179
frère m 22
frette m 258
frire 67
frise f 300
frisé 39
frit à la poêle m / frite à la poêle f 159
frites f 154
froid m / froide f 286, 321
fromage m 136, 156
fromage à la crème m 136
fromage à pâte molle m 136
fromage à pâte pressée cuite m 136
fromage à pâte pressée non cuite m 136
fromage à pâte semi-molle m 136
fromage blanc m 136
fromage de chèvre m 142
fromage frais m 136
fromage frais à tartiner m 136
fromage râpé m 136
froncement de sourcils m 25
front m 14
frontal m 16, 242
fronton m 301
fruit m 126
fruit à pain m 124
fruit confit m 129
fruit de la passion m 128
fruits m 107, 128, 157
fruits à noyau m 126
fruits de me m 121
fruit secs m 156
fruits en bocaux m 135
fruits tropicaux m 129
fumé m / fumée f 118, 121, 143, 159
fumée f 95
fumer 112
fusain m 275
fuseau m 277
fusée éclairante f 240
fuselage m 210
fusible m 60
fusil m 118

G

Gabon 317
gagnant m / gagnante f 273
gagner 273
galaxie f 280
galerie f 198
galerie à vélo f 207
gallon m 311
galop m 243
galvanisé 79
gamba f 121
Gambie 317
gamme f 256
gant f 246
gant m 224, 228, 233, 236
gant isolant m 69
gants m 36
gants de boxe m 237
gants de jardinage m 89
garage m 58, 199
garçon m 23
garde-boue m 205
garde-côtes m/f 217
gardien de but m / gardienne de but f 222, 224
gardien de guichet m / gardienne de guichet f 225
gardien de prison m / gardienne de prison f 181
gare f 208
garer 195
gare routière f 197
garniture f 140, 155
gâteau au chocolat m 140
gâteau d'anniversaire m 141
gâteau de mariage m 141
gâteau de miel m 134
gâteaux de fête m 141
gaufres f 157
gaze f 47
gazeuse 144
gazonner 90
gel m 38, 109, 287
gel douche m 73
gélule f 109
gemmes f 288
gencive f 50
gendre m 22
gêné m / gênée f 25
génération f 23
génératrice f 60
genou m 12
genouillère f 205, 227
genres de pêche m 245
genres de plantes m 86
gens 12
géographie f 162
géomètre m/f 188
géométrie f 165
Géorgie 318

gerbera m 110
germe de soja m 122
germoir m 89
geyser m 285
Ghana 317
gibier à plume m 119
gigot m 119
gilet m 33
gilet de sauvetage m 240
gin m 145
gingembre m 125, 133
gin tonic m 151
girafe f 291
giroflée f 110
givre m 287
glaçage m 141
glace f 120, 137, 149, 287
glacier m 284
glaçon m 151, 287
glaïeul m 110
glande f 19
glaucome m 51
glisser 229
glissière de sécurité f 195
gneiss m 288
goéland f 292
golf m 232
golfeur m / golfeuse f 232
gomme f 163
gong m 257
gorge f 19, 284
gorille m 291
gospel m 259
gothique 301
gouache f 274
gousse f 122, 125
gouttes m 109
gouttière f 58
gouvernail m 241
gouverne f 210
goyave f 128
GPS m 201
grain m 122, 130
grain de beauté m 14
grain de moutarde m 131
grain de poivre m 132
graine f 122, 130
graine de carvi f 131
graine de courge f 131
graine de sésame f 131
graine de tourneso f 131
graines f 88, 131
graines de fenouil f 133
graines de soja 131
grains m 144
gramme m 310
grand m / grande f 321
grand bassin m 239
grande aiguille f 304
grande cisaille f 88
grande cuiller f 68
grand lit m 71
grand magasin m 105
grand-mère f 22

grand-père m 22
grands-parents m 23
grand-voile f 240
grange f 182
granit m 288
graphite m 289
gras 39, 41
gras m 119
gratte-ciel m 299, 300
grattoir m 82
gravier m 88
gravure f 275
Grèce 316
gréement m 240
green m 232
greffer 91
grêle f 286
Grenade 314
grenade f 128
grenat m 288
grenier m 58
grenouille f 294
grenouillère f 30
grès m 288
griffe f 291, 293
gril m 69
grillé m / grillée f 129, 159
grille de refroidissement f 69
grille-pain m 66
griller 67
grippe f 44
gris 39, 274
Groenland 314
gros m / grosse f 321
groseille f 127
groseille à maquereau f 127
groseille blanche f 127
gros intestin m 18
gros orteil m 15
grossesse f 52
grue f 187, 216, 292
grue de caméra f 178
Guatemala 314
guêpe f 295
guêpière f 35
guichet m 96, 209, 216, 225
guichetier m / guichetière f 96
guide m 104
guide de fil m 276
guide touristique m/f 260
guidon m 207
guimauve f 113
guindeau m 214
Guinée 317
Guinée-Bissau 317
Guinée équatoriale 317
guirlande de fleurs f 111
guitare électrique f 258
guitariste m/f 258
Guyane 315
Guyane française 315
gymnaste m/f 235

français

français

français

Sao Tomé-et-
Principe 317
sapeurs-pompiers m /
sapeuses-pompières
f 95
saphir m 288
Sardaigne 316
sardine f 120, 266
sas d'équipage m 281
satellite m 281
satsuma f 126
Saturne m 280
sauce f 135, 143, 155
sauce soja f 135
saucisse f 155, 157
saucisses m 118
saucisson piquant
m 142
sauf 228
sauge f 133
saule m 296
saumon m 120
sauna m 250
saut m 237,
243, 247
saut à la corde m 251
saut à la perche m 234
saut à l'élastique m 248
sauté m / sautée f 159
sauté m 158
saut de cheval m 235
saut en hauteur m 235
saut en longueur m 235
saut en parachute
m 248
sauter 227
sauterelle f 295
sauvegarder 177
sauveteur m /
sauveteuse f 265
savon m 73
saxophone m 257
scalpel m 81, 167
scanner m 48
scanneur m 176
scarabée m 295
scène f 254
schiste m 288
scie à chantourner f 81
scie à main f 89
scie à métaux f 81
scie à tenon f 81
scie circulaire f 78
scie égoïne f 81
science f 166
sciences f 162
sciences économiques
f 169
sciences politiques f 169
scientifique m/f 190
scier 79
scie sauteuse f 78
scooter m 205
score m 220, 273
scorpion m 295
scotch m 173
scotch à l'eau m 151
scrabble m 272
scrotum m 21
sculpter 79

sculpteur m / sculptrice
f 191
sculpture f 275
sculpture sur bois f
275
seau m 77, 82, 265
seau à glace m 150
sec 39, 41, 145, 286
sec m / sèche f 130,
321
sécateur m 89
s'échauffer 251
séché m / séchée f 129,
130, 143, 159
sèche-cheveux m 38
sèche-linge m 76
sécher 38, 76
seconde f 304
se coucher 71
secouriste m/f 94
secrétariat m 168
section f 282
sécurité f 75, 240
sécurité m 212
sécurité enfant f 75
sédatif m 109
sédimentaire 288
se faire des amis 26
se lever 71, 139
seiche f 121
sein m 12
seize 308
seizième 309
sel m 64, 152
sélecteur de point m
276
selfie m 271
selle f 204, 206, 242
selle amazone f 242
semaine f 306
semaine dernière f 307
semaine prochaine f
307
se marier 26
semelle f 37
semer 90, 183
se mettre à quai 217
semis m 91
semoule f 130
s'endormir 71
Sénégal 317
se noyer 239
sensible 41
sens interdit 195
sentier m 262
s'entraîner 251
sept 308
sept cents 308
septembre m 306
septième 309
Serbie 316
se réveiller 71
seringue f 109, 167
serpent m 293
serpillière f 77
serre f 85
serre-joint m 78
serre-tête m 38
serrure de sécurité m 75
serrure f 59

serrurerie f 115
serveur m 176
serveur m / serveuse f
152, 191
service m 231
service après-vente m
104, 175
service compris 152
service de blanchisserie
f 101
service de ménage
m 101
service de prêt m 168
service des ressources
humaines m 175
service de santé m 168
service de soins
intensifs m 48
service des ventes m
175
service d'étage m 101
service juridique m 175
service marketing m
175
service non compris
152
services d'urgence
m 94
services m 49, 94, 101
serviette f 37, 65, 73
serviette de bain m 73
serviette de plage f 265
serviette en papier f 154
serviette hygiénique f
108
serviettes m 73
servir 64, 231
set m 230
set de table m 64
s'évanouir 25, 44
shaker à cocktails m
150
shampoing m 38
sherry m 145
shiatsu m 54
shooter 223
short m 33
short de bain 264
shot m 151
Sibérie f 313
Sicile 316
siècle m 307
siège m 64, 209,
210, 242
siège arrière m
200, 204
siège d'enfant m
198, 207
siège du conducteur
m 196
siège social m 175
Sierra Leone 317
signal m 209
signature f 98
silence m 256
silencieux 321
silencieux m 203, 204
silencieux m /
silencieuse f 321
silex m 288

sillon m 183
silo m 182
simple 151
simple m 230
Singapour 319
singe m 291
sinus m 19
sirène f 94
sirop m 109
sirop d'érable m 134
site web m 177
six 308
six cents 308
sixième 309
skateboard m 249, 263
ski m 241, 246
ski alpin m 247
ski de fond m 247
skieur / skieuse f 246
ski nautique m 241
slalom m 247
slalom géant m 247
slice m 230
slip m 33, 35
slip de bain m 238
Slovaquie 316
Slovénie 316
smartphone m 99, 176
smash m 231
SMS m 99
snack bar m 148
snowboard m 247
société f 175
sœur f 22
soie m 277
soigner 91
soin du visage m 41
soins de bébé m 74
soins de bébés m 104
soins de la peau m 108
soins dentaires m 108
soins esthétiques m 41
soir m 305
soixante 308
soixante-dix 308
soixante-dixième 309
soixantième 309
sol m 62, 71
sol argileux m 85
sol calcaire m 85
soldat m / soldate f
189
sole f 120
soleil m 280, 286
solides m 164
sol limoneux m 85
sol sableux m 85
soluble m/f 109
solution désinfectante
f 51
solution nettoyante f 51
solvant m 83
Somalie 317
sombre m/f 321
sommet m 164
sommier m 71
somnifère m 109
son m 130
sonate f 256
sonde f 50

sonnette f 59, 197
sorbet m 141
sortie f 61, 75, 210
Soudan 317
Soudan du Sud 317
souder 79
soudure m 79
soufflé m 158
souffler 141
soufre m 289
soupape de sûreté f
61
soupe f 153
soupirer 25
sourcil m 14, 51
sourire m 25
souris f 176, 290
sous 320
sous-exposé 271
sous-marin m 215
sous-sol m 58, 91
sous tension 60
soustraire 165
sous-vêtements m 32
sous-vêtements
thermiques m 267
soute à bagages f 196
soutien-gorge m 35
soutien-gorge
d'allaitement m 53
soutien-gorge de sport
m 35
souvenirs m 260
souvent 320
sparadrap m 47
spatule f 68, 167, 246
spécialiste m/f 49
spécialités m 152
spectateurs m 233
spermatozoïde m 20
sphère f 164
sports m 220
sports aquatiques
m 241
sports de combat
m 236
sports d'hiver m 247
spray m 109
sprinter m / sprinteuse
f 234
squash m 231
squat m 251
squelette m 17
Sri Lanka 318
stabilisateurs m 207
stade m 223
station de charge f 268
station de radio f 179
station de taxis f 213
station-service f 199
station spatiale f 281
statue f 261
statuette f 260
steeple-chase m 243
stepper m 250
sténographe m/f 181
stéréo 269
stérile 20, 47
stérilet m 21
sternum m 17

français

français

Index anglais • English index

english

english

brunette 39
brush 38, 40, 77, 83, 274
brush v 38, 50
Brussels sprout 123
bubble bath 73
bucket 77, 82
buckle 36
bud 111, 297
buffet 152
build v 186
buildings 299
bulb 86
Bulgaria 316
bull 185
bulldog clip 173
bulletin board 173
bull-nose pliers 80
bullseye 273
bumper 198
bun 39, 139, 140, 155
bunch 111
bungalow 58
bungee jumping 248
bunker 232
Bunsen burner 166
buoy 217
burger 154
burger bar 154
burger meal 154
burglar alarm 58
burglary 94
Burkina Faso 317
burn 46
burner 61, 67
Burundi 317
bus 196
bus driver 190
business 175
business class 211
business deal 175
business lunch 175
businessman 175
business partner 24
business suit 32
business trip 175
businesswoman 175
bus shelter 197
bus station 197
bus stop 197, 299
bus ticket 197
bustier 35
busy 99
butcher 118, 188
butcher shop 114
butter 137, 156
butter beans 131
buttercup 297
butterfly 239, 295
buttermilk 137
butternut squash 125
buttock 13
button 32

buttonhole 32
buttress 301
by 320
by airmail 98
bytes 176

C

cab 95
cabbage 123
cabin 210, 214
cabinet 66
cable 79, 207
cable car 246
cable television 269
cactus 87
caddy 233
café 148, 262
cafeteria 168
cake pan 69
cakes 140
calcite 289
calcium 109
calculator 165
calendar 306
calf 13, 16, 185
calyx 297
Cambodia 319
camcorder 269
camel 291
Camembert 142
camera 178, 260
camera case 271
camera crane 178
camera operator 178
camera phone 270
Cameroon 317
camisole 35
camp v 266
camp bed 266
camper 266
camper van 266
campfire 266
campground 266
camping 266
camping stove 267
campus 168
can 145, 311
Canada 314
canary 292
candied fruit 129
candy 107
candy store 113
cane 91
canes 89
canine 50
canned drink 154
canned food 107
canning jar 135
canoe 214
canola oil 135
can opener 68
canter 243
canvas 274
cap 36

capacity 311
Cape gooseberry 128
capers 143
capital 315
capoeira 237
cappuccino 148
capsize v 241
capsule 109
captain 94, 214
car 198, 200, 202
car accident 203
caramel 113
caraway seed 131
card 27
cardamom 132
cardboard 275
cardigan 32
cardiology 49
cardiovascular 19
card reader 97
cards 273
cargo 216
Caribbean Sea 312
carnation 110
carnival 27
carpenter 188
carpentry bits 80
carpet 71
car rental 213
carriage race 243
carrier 75, 204
carrot 124
carry-on luggage 211, 213
car seat 198
car stereo 201
cart 100, 208, 213
cartilage 17
carton 311
cartoon 178
cartwheel 235
carve v 79
carving fork 68
car wash 199
case 51, 269
cash v 97
cashew 129, 151
cash register 106, 150
casino 261
Caspian Sea 313
cassava 124
casserole dish 69
cast 254
cast v 245
castle 300
casual wear 33
cat 290
catamaran 215
cataract 51
catch v 220, 227, 229, 245
catcher 229

caterpillar 295
cathedral 300
catheter 53
cattail 86
cauliflower 124
cave 284
CD player 268
cedar 296
celebration 140
celebration cakes 141
celebrations 27
celeriac 124
celery 122
cell 94, 181
cello 256
cell phone 99
cement 186
cement mixer 186
center 164
centerboard 241
center circle 222, 224, 226
center field 228
centimeter 310
centipede 295
Central America 314
Central African Republic 317
century 307
CEO 175
ceramic stovetop 66
cereal 130, 156
cervical cap 21
cervical vertebrae 17
cervix 20, 52
cesarean section 52
chain 36, 206
chair 64
chair v 174
chairlift 246
chalk 85, 288
chamber 283
chamomile tea 149
champagne 145
championship 230
change a tire v 203
change channel v 269
change gears v 207
change purse 37
changing mat 74
changing table 74
channel 178
charcoal 266, 275
charge 94, 180
charging cable 176, 198
chart 48
chassis 203
cheap 321
check 152
checker 106
checkers 272
check in v 212

check-in desk 213
checking account 96
checkout 106
checkup 50
cheddar 142
cheek 14
cheerleader 220
cheese 136, 156
chef 152, 190
chef's hat 190
chemistry 162
cherry 126
cherry tomato 124
chess 272
chessboard 272
chest 12
chestnut 129
chest of drawers 70
chest press 251
chewing gum 113
chick 185
chicken 119, 185
chicken coop 185
chicken nuggets 155
chicken pox 44
chicken sandwich 155
chickpeas 131
chicory 122
child 23, 31
childbirth 53
child lock 75
children 23
children's clothing 30
children's department 104
children's ward 48
child seat 207
child's meal 153
Chile 315
chill 44
chili pepper 124, 143
chili powder 132, 143
chimney 58
chin 14
china 105
China 318
chip v 233
chiropractic 54
chisel 81, 275
chives 133
chocolate 113
chocolate bar 113
chocolate cake 140
chocolate chip 141
chocolate-covered 140
chocolate milkshake 149
chocolate spread 135
choir 301
choke v 47
chop 119, 237
chopsticks 158

english

english

english

english

little, a 320
little finger 15
little toe 15
live 60, 178
liver 18, 118
live rail 209
livestock 182, 185
living room 62
lizard 293
load v 76
loaf 139
loan 96, 168
lob 231
lobby 100, 255
lobster 121, 295
lock 59, 207
lockers 239
locksmith 115
loganberry 127
logo 31
log on v 177
loin 121
lollipop 113
long 32
long-distance bus 196
long-grain 130
long-handled shears 88
longitude 283
long jump 235
loom 277
loose-leaf tea 144
lose v 273
loser 273
lot, a 320
love 230
low 321
luge 247
luggage 100, 198, 213
luggage department 104
luggage hold 196
luggage rack 209
lug nuts 203
lumbar vertebrae 17
lumber 187
lunar module 281
lunch 64
lunch menu 152
lung 18
lunge 251
lupines 297
lure 244
Luxembourg 316
lychee 128
lymphatic 19
lyrics 259

M

macadamia 129
mace 132
machinery 187
macramé 277
Madagascar 317
magazine 112

magazines 107
magma 283
magnesium 109
magnet 167
maid service 101
mailbag 189, 190
mailbox 58
mail carrier 98, 190
main course 153
mainsail 240
make a will v 26
make friends v 26
make the bed v 71
makeup 40
making bread 138
malachite 289
Malawi 317
Malaysia 319
Maldives 318
male 12, 13, 21
Mali 317
mallet 275
Malta 316
malted milk 144
malt vinegar 135
mammals 290
man 23
manager 24, 174
Manchego 142
mane 242
mango 128
manhole 299
manicure 41
mantle 282
manual 200
map 261
maple 296
maple syrup 134
maracas 257
marathon 234
marble 288
March 306
margarine 137
marina 217
marinated 143, 159
marine fishing 245
marjoram 133
mark v 227
market 115
marketing department 175
marketing executive 189
marmalade 134, 156
Mars 280
marshmallow 113
martial arts 237
martini 151
marzipan 141
mascara 40
mashed 159
masher 68
mask 189, 228, 236, 239, 249

masking tape 83
masonry bit 80
massage 54
mast 240
master's 169
mat 54, 235
match 230
material 276
materials 79, 187
maternity 49
maternity ward 48
math 162, 164
matte 83, 271
mattress 70, 74
Mauritania 317
Mauritius 317
May 306
maybe 322
mayonnaise 135
MDF 79
meadow 285
meal 64
measles 44
measure 150, 151
measure v 310
measurements 165
measuring cup 69, 311
measuring spoon 109
meat 107, 118
meatballs 158
meat hook 118
meat pies 143
meat tenderizer 68
mechanic 188, 203
mechanics 202
medals 235
media 178
median strip 194
medical examination 45
medication 109
medicine 109, 169
medicine cabinet 72
meditation 54
Mediterranean Sea 313
meeting 174
meeting room 174
melody 259
melon 127
memory 176
memory stick 176
menstruation 20
menswear 105
menu 148, 153, 154
menubar 177
mercury 289
Mercury 280
meringue 140
mesosphere 286
metacarpal 17
metal 79
metal bit 80
metals 289
metamorphic 288

metatarsal 17
meteor 280
meter 310
Mexico 314
mezzanine 254
mica 289
microphone 179, 258
microscope 167
microwave oven 66
middle finger 15
middle lane 194
midnight 305
midpoint line 226
midwife 53
migraine 44
mile 310
milk 136, 156
milk v 183
milk carton 136
milk chocolate 113
milk shake 137, 149
millennium 307
millet 130
milligram 310
milliliter 311
millimeter 310
minerals 289
mineral water 144
minibar 101
minibus 197
minivan 199
mint 133, 133
mint tea 149
minus 165
minute 304
minute hand 304
minutes 174
mirror 40, 71, 167
miscarriage 52
missile 211
Miss 23
mist 287
miter block 81
mittens 30
mix v 67, 138
mixing bowl 66, 69
mixing desk 179
moat 300
mobile 74
mobile data 99
model 169, 190
modeling tool 275
model-making 275
moisturizer 41
molar 50
molding 63
Moldova 316
mole 14
Monaco 316
Monday 306
money 97
Mongolia 318
monitor 53, 172
monkey 291

Monopoly 272
monorail 208
monsoon 287
Montenegro 316
month 306
monthly 307
monument 261
moon 280
moonstone 288
moor v 217
mooring 217
mop 77
morning 305
Morocco 317
mortar 68, 167, 187
mortgage 96
mosque 300
mosquito 295
mosquito net 267
moth 295
mother 22
mother-in-law 23
motion-sickness pills 109
motor 88
motorcycle 204
motorcycle racing 249
motocross 249
mountain 284
mountain bike 206
mountain range 282
mouse 176, 290
mousse 141
mouth 14
mouth guard 237
mouthwash 72
move 273
movies 255
movie set 179
movie theater 255, 299
mow v 90
Mozambique 317
mozzarella 142
Mr. 23
Mrs. 23
Ms. 23
muffin 140
muffin pan 69
muffler 203, 204
mug 65
mulch v 91
multigrain bread 139
multiply v 165
multivitamins 109
mumps 44
mung beans 131
muscles 16
museum 261
mushroom 125
music 162
musical 255
musical score 255
musical styles 259
musician 191

english

english

run *v* 229
runner bean 122
runway 212
rush hour 209
Russian Federation 318
rutabaga 125
Rwanda 317
rye bread 138

S

sad 25
saddle 206, 242
safari park 262
safe 228
safety 75, 240
safety barrier 246
safety goggles 81, 167
safety pin 47
saffron 132
sage 133
Sahara Desert 313
sail 215, 241
sailboat 215
sailing 240
sailor 189
sake 145
salad 149
salamander 294
salami 142
salary 175
salesclerk 104
sales department 175
salesperson 188
salmon 120
salon 115
salt 64, 152
salted 121, 129, 137, 143
sand 85, 264
sand *v* 82
sandal 37
sandals 31
sandbox 263
sandcastle 265
sander 78
sandpaper 81, 83
sandstone 288
sandwich 155
sandwich counter 143
sanitary napkin 108
San Marino 316
São Tomé and Principe 317
sapphire 288
sardine 120
Sardinia 316
satellite 281
satellite dish 268
satsuma 126
Saturday 306
Saturn 280
sauce 143, 155

saucepan 69
sauces 135
Saudi Arabia 318
sauna 250
sausage 155, 157
sausages 118
sauté *v* 67
save *v* 177, 223
savings 96
savings account 96
savory 155
saw *v* 79
saxophone 257
scaffolding 186
scale 45, 69, 98, 118, 121, 166, 256, 294, 310
scaled 121
scales 293
scallion 125
scallop 121
scalp 39
scalpel 167
scan 48, 52
scanner 106, 176
scarecrow 184
scared 25
scarf 31, 36
schedule 197, 209, 261
schist 288
scholarship 169
school 162, 299
school backpack 162
school bus 196
schools 169
science 162, 166
science fiction movie 255
scientist 190
scissors 38, 47, 82, 276
scoop 149
scooter 205
score 220, 256, 273
score a goal *v* 223
scoreboard 225
scorpion 295
scotch and water 151
Scotland 316
Scrabble 272
scrape *v* 77
screen 97, 176, 255, 269
screw 80
screwdriver 80, 151
screwdriver bits 80
script 254
scrotum 21
scrub *v* 7
scuba diving 239
seahorse 294
seat 61

seat belt 211
seafood 121
seaplane 211
second floor 104
secondhand store 115
sedan 199
seed 128, 127
seeds 131
self-defense 237
selfie 271
self-rising flour 139
self-tanning lotion 41
server 152, 191
service charge included 152
service charge not included 152
services 101
sesame seed 131
sesame seed oil 134
set 178, 230, 254
set *v* 38
set sail *v* 217
set the alarm *v* 71
set the table *v* 64
seven 308
seven hundred 308
seventeen 308
seventeenth 309
seventh 309
seventieth 309
seventy 308
sew *v* 277
sewing basket 276
sewing machine 276
sexually transmitted infection 20
shade 41
shade plant 87
shallot 125
shallow end 239
shampoo 38
shapes 164
share price 97
shares 97
shark 294
sharp 256
shaving 73
shaving foam 73
shears 89
shed 85
sheep 185
sheep farm 183
sheer curtain 63
sheet 71, 74, 241
shelf 66, 106
shell 129, 137, 265, 293
shelled 129
sherbet 141
sherry 145
shiatsu 54
shield 88

shin 12
shingle 58
ship 214
shipyard 217
shirt 33
shock 47
shocked 25
shoe department 104
shoes 34, 37
shoot *v* 223, 227
shopping 104
shopping bag 106
shopping center 104
short 32, 321
short-grain 130
short haircut 39
shorts 30, 33
shot 151
shotput 234
shoulder 13, 194
shoulder bag 37
shoulder blade 17
shoulder pad 35
shoulder strap 37
shout *v* 25
shovel 88, 187, 265
shower 72, 286
shower block 266
shower curtain 72
shower door 72
shower gel 73
shower head 72
showjumping 243
shredder 172
shrimp 121
shuffle *v* 273
shutter 58
shut-off valve 61
shutter release 270
shuttle bus 197
shuttlecock 231
shy 25
Siberia 313
Sicily 316
sick 321
side 164
side-by-side refrigerator 67
sidedeck 240
side dish 153
side effects 109
sideline 220, 226, 230
side mirror 198
side plate 65
sidesaddle 242
side street 299
sidewalk 298
sidewalk café 148
Sierra Leone 317
sieve 68, 89
sift *v* 91, 138
sigh *v* 25
sightseeing 260

signal 209
signature 98
silk 277
silo 182
silt 85
silver 235, 289
simmer *v* 67
Singapore 319
singer 191
single 151
single-family 58
single room 100
singles 230
sink 38, 50, 61, 66, 72
sinker 244
sinus 19
sippy cup 74
siren 94
sirloin steak 119
sister 22
sister-in-law 23
site 266
sites available 266
site manager's office 266
sit-up 251
six 308
six hundred 308
sixteen 308
sixteenth 309
sixth 309
sixtieth 309
sixty 308
skate 120, 247, 294
skate *v* 224
skateboard 249
skateboarding 249, 263
skein 277
skeleton 17
sketch 275
sketch pad 275
skewer 68
ski 241, 246
ski boot 246
skier 246
skiing 246
ski jacket 246
ski jump 247
skim milk 136
skin 14, 119
skin care 108
skinned 121
ski pole 246
skipping 251
skirt 30, 34
ski run 246
ski slope 246
skull 17
skydiving 248
skyscraper 299, 300
slalom 247
slate 288
sledding 247

english

english

english

remerciements • acknowledgments

DORLING KINDERSLEY would like to thank senior picture researchers Deepak Negi and Sumedha Chopra, assistant picture researcher Samrajkumar S, and proofreaders Diana Vowles, Heather Wilcox, Catharine Robertson, Chuck Hutchinson, Sam Cooke, Ruth Raisenberger.

The publisher would like to thank the following for their kind permission to reproduce their photographs:

Abbreviations key: (a-above; b-below/bottom; c-centre; f-far; l-left; r-right; t-top)

123RF.com: Aicandy 188fbr; Andriy Popov 34tl; Arthousestudio 265fcla; Astemmer 208c; avigatorphotographer 216bl; Brad Wynnyk 172bc; Cladanifer 25fclb; Daniel Ernst 179tc; Hongqi Zhang 24cla; 175cr; Ingvar Bjork 60c; Koonsiri 5cla, 92-93; Kobby Dagan 259c; Kritchanut 25ftl; Lightfieldstudios 35tr; Liubov Vadimovna (Luba) Nel 39cla; Ljupco Smokovski 75crb; Olegtroino 176fcl; Olga Popova 33c; Peopleimages12 41tl; Robert Churchill 94c; Roman Gorielov 33bc; Ruslan Kudrin 35bc, 35br; Subbotina 39cra; Sutichak Yachaingkham 39tc; Tarzhanova 37tc; Vitaly Valua 39tl; Wilawan Khasawong 75cb; **Action Plus:** 224bc; **Alamy Images:** 154t; Alex Segre 150t; A.T. Willett 287bcl; Alex Segre 105ca; Andrew Barker 195fcl; Ambrophoto 24cra; Art Directors & TRIP / Helene Rogers 115bl; artpartner-images.com 181tc; Ben Queenborough 213crb; Boaz Rottem 209cr; Cultura RM 33r; Bernhard Classen 97bc; David Burton 177clb; Carl DeAbreu 264t; Cavan Images 247fcla; Chicken Strip 112fbr; Chris George 271bc; Destina 176crb; Dorling Kindersley Ltd 266t; Dorling Kindersley Ltd / Vanessa Davies 74ftr; dpa picture alliance 112t; Doug Houghton 107fbr; Doug Houghton 213fclb; Gianni Muratore 195ftr; Henri Martin 182ca; Hideo Kurihara 212t; Hugh Threlfall 35tl; Hugh Threlfall 268bl; Ian Townsley 260cr; Ifeelstock 96cr; Incamerastock / ICP-UK 112fcrb; Issac Rose 54fcr; Jeff Gilbert 213fcrb; keith morris 178c; Majestic Media Ltd 224bc; Thomas 221br, 223crb; Nikreates 268crb; Nathaniel Noir 114bl; MBI 175tl; Michael Foyle 184bl; Olaf Doering 213br; Oleksiy Maksymenko 105bc; Paul Maguire 186t; Pally 294bl; Paul Weston 168br; Prisma Bildagentur AG 246b; Simone Hogan 241cla; Radharc Images 197tr; Ruslan Kudrin 176tl; Sasa Huzjak 258t; Sergey Kravchenko 37ca; Sergio Azenha 270bc; Stock Connection 287bcr; tarczas 35cr; Ton Koene 213cra; Transport Infrastructures / Paul White 216t; Trekandshoot 194c; Robert Stainforth 98tl; vitaly suprun 176cl; Wavebreak Media Ltd 39cl, 174b, 175tr; Wavebreakmedia Ltd IP-200810 234fcl; **Allsport/Getty Images:** 238cl; **Alvey and Towers:** 241cr; **Anthony Blake Photo Library:** Charlie Stebbings 114cl; **Arcaid:** John Edward Linden 301bl; Martine Hamilton Knight, Architects: Richard Bryant 301br; **Argos:** Nick Couchman 148cr; **Bosch:** 76tc, 76tcl; **Camera Press:** 38tr; 257cr; Barry J. Holmes 148br; Jane Hanger 159cr; Mary Germanou 259bc; **Corbis:** 78b; Anna Clopet 247tr; Ariel Skelley / Blend Images 52l; Bettmann 181tr; Bo Zauders 156t; Bob Winsett 247cbl; Brian Bailey 247br; Craig Aurness 215bl; David H.Wells 249cbr; Dennis Marsico 274bl; Dimitri Lundt 236bc; Duomo 211tl; Gail Mooney 277ctcr; George Lepp 248c; Gerald Nowak 239b; Gunter Marx 248cr; Jack Hollingsworth 231bl; James L. Amos 247bl, 191ctr, 220bcr; Jan Butchofsky 277cbc; Johnathan Blair 243cr; Jose F. Poblete 191br; Jose Luis Pelaez.Inc 153tc; Karl Weatherly 220bl, 247tcr; Kelly Mooney Photography 259tl; Kevin Fleming 249bc; Kevin R. Morris 105tr, 243tl, 243tc; Kim Sayer 249fcr; Lynn Goldsmith 258t; Macduff Everton 231bcl; Mark Gibson 249bl; Mark L. Stephenson 249tcl; Mike King 247cbl; Pablo Corral 115bc; 249ctcl; Paul J. Sutton 224c, 224br; Phil Schermeister 227b, 248tr; R. W Jones 309; Rick Doyle 241ctr; Robert Holmes 97br, 277ctc; Roger Ressmeyer 169tr; Russ Schleipman 229t; The Purcell Team 211ctr; Wally McNamee 220bc, 220bcl, 224bl; Wavebreak Media Ltd 191bc; Yann Arhus-Bertrand 249tl; **Depositphotos Inc:** Londondepositd 262br; **Demetrio Carrasco / Dorling Kindersley (c) Herge / Les Editions Casterman:** 112ccl; **Dixons:** 270cl, 270cr, 270bl, 270bcl, 270bc, 270ccr; **Dorling Kindersley:** Banbury Museum 35c; Five Napkin Burger 152t; **Dreamstime.com:** Adempercem 197cb; Akesin 191tl; 191cr; Aleksandar Todorovic 300bl; Anan Budtviengpunth 299cra; Andersastphoto 176tc; Andrey Popov 191bl, 55fcra, 190ftr; Anna Eremeeva 82crb; Anna Griessel 25cra; Anna Tolipova 277ftr; Anatoliy Samara 311tc; Anton Matveev 2bl; Arenaphotouk 209tr; Arne9001 190tl; Arnel Manalang 195fbr; Artzzz 201b; Avagyanleon 269cla; Birgit Reitz Hofmann 144ca; Bonandbon Dw 154bc; Bright 199tr; Chaoss 26c; Chernetskaya 60tc, 240tc; Christian Offenberg 99ftl; Colicaranica 210t; Dimaberkut 200cr; Dmitry Markov 5fcla, 56-57; Dvmsimages 196bc; Dzmitry Rishchuk 152t; Eakkachai Halang 101ftl; Ekostsov 198fbl; Elena Masiutkina 105fcrb; Ellesi 197br; Evgeny Karandaev 145br; Exiledphoto 1ca (Golf Balls), 5fcrb, 218-219; Gradts 76ftr; Grigor Ivanov 82bl; Gutaper 176br; Hasan Can Balcioglu 261c; Hxdbzxy 5cra, 102-103; Hywit Dimyadi 184clb; Iakov Filimonov 115br; Ivan Danik 4fcrb, 146-147; Ivan Katsarov 201t; Ilfede 215clb; Innicco 269tc; Isselee 292fcrb; Jamesteohart 290br; Jiri Hera 269c; Joe Sohm 259tr; Johncox1958 243ca; Kaspars Grinvalds 172cfr; Kenny Tong 5tr, 10-11; Kineticimagery 5bl, 302-303; Konstantinos Moraitis 199tl; Lah 249crb; Larry Gevert 1ca (peppers), 5fcra, 116-117; Leonid Andronov 208clb; Leo Daphne 145cb; Leen Beunens 299tl; Lulia Diakova 15tr; Natalia Bratslavsky 101cl; Natvishenka 269tr; Njnightsky 70bl; Nuwan Fernandez 177tr; Maciej Bledowski 95c, 206br; Madrugadaverde 298t; Maksim Toome 199ftr; Maniapixel 215tr; Matthias Ziegler 191ftl; Mholod 4fcra, 42-43; Micha Rojek 177tc; Miff32 197bl; Mike Kiev 199cr; Mikeal Keal 269ca; Mohamed Osama 75fbl; Monkey Business Images 26clb, 100t, 169tl; Monticello 145ftl; Olena Turovtseva 216br; Olga Plugatar 271clb (X2), 271fcla; Pac 268clb; Paolo De Santis 261ftr; Patricia Hofmeester

233cra; Paul Michael Hughes 162tr; Petro Perutskyy 199bl; Phanuwatn 269cl; Photka 213fcra; Ponomarencko 152cr; Roza 300tc; Ryzhov Sergey 138t; Schamie 176cl; Seanlockephotography 189clb; Sean Pavone 301tl; Shariff Che\'' Sjors737 277cb; Serghei Starus 190bc; Sergey Galushko 77ftl; Sergey Tolmachyov 270br; Serezniy 48crb; Steafpong 87bl; Sutsaiy 66bl; Takcrane3 198t; Tatiana3337 1ca (multicolor); Theerasak Tammachuen 269cr, 5fclb, 160-161; Trak 256t; Tyler Olson 168crb; Vetkit 189fclb; Volodymyr Melnyk 231ca, 235fcrb; Wang Song 250br, 261cr; Wirestock 169tc; Zerbor 296tr; **Education Photos:** John Walmsley 261tl; **Getty Images:** 287tr; 94tr; Corbis Historical / Christopher Pillitz 169cr; George Doyle & Ciaran Griffin 22cr; David Leahy 162tl; DigitalVision / David Leahy 162cla; DigitalVision / Are 227cra; Don Farrall / Digital Vision 176c; Ethan Miller 270bl; Inti St Clair 179bl; Jeff Bottari 236br; LightRocket / SOPA Images 227ftl; Sean Justice / Digital Vision 24br; The Image Bank / Michael Dunning 235cra; **Getty Images / iStock:** ake1150sb 154bl, AndyOman 304 (Digital Clock X3), Archideaphoto 268t, Babayev 76fcrb, Bluesky85 213tl, Bluestocking 268cb, Bonetta 66fbr, Svetlana Borisova 286cr, Bulgnn 112br, Hadzhi Hristo Chorbadzhi 260tl, DigitalVision Vectors / youngID 96cl, E+ / Adamkaz 206bl, E+ / Aldomurillo 189cra, E+ / AnVr 144bl, E+ / BraunS 231br, E+ / Dean Mitchell 55ftr, E+ / FG Trade 179ftl, E+ / Fly View Productions 96t, E+ / Ivan Pantic 206bcr, E+ / Joel Carillet 215br, E+ / JohnnyGreig 104t, E+ / Jondpatton 196br, E+ / Kali9 186bl, 190clb, E+ / Lorado 115bc, E+ / Mbbirdy 66fclb, E+ / Pagadesign 97tr, E+ / Petko Ninov 198fbr, E+ / Satoshi-K 259crb, E+ / SDI Productions 55fbl, E+ / SolStock 221clb, E+ / South_agency 114br, E+ / Studiocasper 270tc, E+ / Sturti 186bc, E+ / Tashi-Delek 179ftr, E+ / Tempura 48clb, E+ / Tolgart 34br, FamVeld 246tr, Farakos 176cr, FG Trade 188fbl, Gannet77 96cc, Grinvalds 99cr, Gumpanat 97cl, Kckate16 188fcla, Kommercialize 208cb, Leedsn 241cra, Sompong Lekhawattana 197tl, LeventKonuk 76cr, Liz Leyden 115tc, LightfieldStudios 169cl, Andrii Lysenko 114tl, Karan Mathur 191cra, MicroStockHub 96clb, Mladn61 196cla, 196-197cca, Moumita Mondal 27fcr, Monkeybusinessimages 49crb, Yaman Mutart 105bl, Nojman 276t, OfirPeretz 195ftl, Prostock-Studio 5clb, 170-171, 188crb, RuslanDashinsky 83tl, Scaliger 208t, Kazuma Seki 188bl, Deepak Sethi 271ftr, SimonSkafar 1ca (Cornflowers), 58t, 278-279, Stocktrek Images 215bl, TACrafts 199cra, Teamtime 210b, The Image Bank / Ryan McVay 247cra, Tilo 69ftr, Toxitz 99cl, Alla Tsyganova 148t, Tunatura 287tc, Universal Images Group / Andia 106t, Andik Tri Witanto 209cra, Chunyip Wong 5crb, 192-193, YakubovAlim 55crb, Zdenkam 23bl, Drazen Zigic 49ftr; **Hulsta:** 70t; **Ideal Standard Ltd:** 72r; **The Image Bank/Getty Images:** 58; **Impact Photos:** Eliza Armstrong 115cr; Philip Achache 246t; **The Interior Archive:** Simon Upton, Architect: Phillippe Starck; **iStockphoto.com:** asterix0597 163tl; EdStock 190br; RichLegg 26bc; **MP Visual. com:** Mark Swallow 202t; **NASA:** 280cr, 280ccl, 281tl; **P A Photos:** 181br; **Plain and Simple Kitchens:** 66t; **Red Consultancy:** Odeon cinemas 257br; **Redferns:** Nigel Crane 259c; **Rex Features:** 106br, 259tc, 259bl, 280b; Charles Ommaney 114tcr; J.F.F Whitehead 243cl; Scott Wiseman 287bl; **Science & Society Picture Library:** Science Museum 202b, Science Photo Library: IBM Research 190cla; NASA 281cr; **Shutterstock.com:** Africa Studio 198bl, Akkalak Aiempradit 26cla, BearFotos 245clb, Ruslan Bercan 213fbl, Comeback Images 24bl, Odin Daniel 214bl, Diamant24 60fclb, Early Spring 100br, Dmytro Falkowskyi 196-197cb, Giuseppe_R 4fbr, 252-253, Kaspars Grinvalds 1ca (Shirts), 5ftr, 28-29, 115clb, Ground Picture 26ftr, 100fbr, Haveseen 264b, HelloRF Zcool 168t, Joseph Hendrickson 59tl, Nigel Jarvis 214bc, Mkfilm 287br, New Africa 71tr, 75ftr, 77cra, Eline Oostingh 215cb, SeventyFour 232bl, Ilya Sviridenko 185fbr, Alla Tsyganova 114fbl, zcw 77ca; **SuperStock:** Ingram Publishing 62; Juanma Aparicio / age fotostock 172t; **Sony:** 268bc; **Neil Sutherland:** 82br, 90t, 118, 188cr, 196t, 299cl, 299bl; **Vauxhall:** 199cl, 200; **Colin Walton:** 99tcl, 401.

DK PICTURE LIBRARY:

Akhil Bahkshi; Patrick Baldwin; Geoff Brightling; British Museum; John Bulmer; Andrew Butler; Joe Cornish; Brian Cosgrove; Andy Crawford and Kit Hougton; Philip Dowell; Alistair Duncan; Gables; Bob Gathany; Norman Hollands; Kew Gardens; Peter James Kindersley; Vladimir Kozlik; Sam Lloyd; London Northern Bus Company Ltd; Tracy Morgan; David Murray and Jules Selmes; Musée Vivant du Cheval, France; Museum of Broadcast Communications; Museum of Natural History; NASA; National History Museum; Norfolk Rural Life Museum; Stephen Oliver; RNLI; Royal Ballet School; Guy Ryecart; Science Museum; Neil Setchfield; Ross Simms and the Winchcombe Folk Police Museum; Singapore Symphony Orchestra; Smart Museum of Art; Tony Souter; Erik Svensson and Jeppe Wikstrom; Sam Tree of Keygrove Marketing Ltd; Barrie Watts; Alan Williams; Jerry Young.

Additional photography by Colin Walton.

Colin Walton would like to thank:

A&A News, Uckfield; Abbey Music, Tunbridge Wells; Arena Mens Clothing, Tunbridge Wells; Burrells of Tunbridge Wells; Gary at Di Marco's; Jeremy's Home Store, Tunbridge Wells; Noakes of Tunbridge Wells; Ottakar's, Tunbridge Wells; Selby's of Uckfield; Sevenoaks Sound and Vision; Westfield, Royal Victoria Place, Tunbridge Wells.

All other images © Dorling Kindersley